HEARTLAND HEARTBEATS

A Country Heritage Story Collection

by

Beth Gibbons

Gotham Books

30 N Gould St.
Ste. 20820, Sheridan, WY 82801
https://gothambooksinc.com/

Phone: 1 (307) 464-7800

© 2023 *Beth Gibbons*. All rights reserved.

No part of this book may be reproduced, stored in a retrieval system, or transmitted by any means without the written permission of the author.

Published by Gotham Books (October 17, 2023)

ISBN: 979-8-88775-495-6 (H)
ISBN: 979-8-88775-493-2 (P)
ISBN: 979-8-88775-494-9 (E)

Because of the dynamic nature of the Internet, any web addresses or links contained in this book may have changed since publication and may no longer be valid.

The views expressed in this work are solely those of the author and do not necessarily reflect the views of the publisher, and the publisher hereby disclaims any responsibility for them.

A man's steps are ordered by the Lord. Proverbs 20:24

This collection of stories is dedicated to my family with love and appreciation for all they mean to me. Thank you, Jerry, Wayne, and Kristi, spouses, and families, all my precious grandchildren and great grandchildren, for being important inspiration in my life. You provide reason for me to get up each morning as you prove that faith and family are of supreme importance. Harold, your father and grandfather, was my husband, love, confidant and best friend. His faith and help gave me the courage to farm, teach and write—alone. Thanks to God who put a desire in me to share stories and what we know of our ancestors.

Inspiration also came from my parents and siblings: Lila, Jim, Ted, Glen and Gene, who maybe unknowingly, provided much material for the contents of this collection of stories. We are close and are thankful for the blessings of family. Thanks to granddaughter, Ashley, for picture scans, Iris Paris, Jo Fisher and others who helped edit. Writings, poems and quotes are by me unless otherwise stated. Memories are mine as I remember and recorded them.

"Believe you can do anything and you can!"

SANDHILLS SERENITY

Sandhills sunsets are a quiet serenity sensation
They thrill our senses with wonderful motivation
Sands whisper in breeze as grasses gently sway
Birds and animals find this is the place to stay

Locals are content to work hours without fears
Little children grow in responsibility and years
Winds whistles through on cold winters' night
We snuggle under big quilts to warm this fright

Sunsets remind us of home and family hearth
They tell of our beloved parents and good earth
'Tis worth looking at grandeur as we gaze about
Appreciating these Sandhills—land of my birth

Table of Contents

Introduction	viii
Robbed!	1
Family	5
Generations Of Family	6
Gibbons Family	8
Gramps' Weather Prognostications	13
Great Grandfather Bryant	14
W. H. Gibbons	15
Aunt Cina	18
Crowell Ancestors	21
Grandma Gibbons	23
Dad's Memories	24
W. W. Weber	26
Grandma Weber	30
Weber Records	33
Jacobina Mack Weber	34
Christopher F Weber:	35
Burris	36
Grandma Paine	37
Aunt Lettie's Cup	41
Great Grandma Paine	43
Obituary	45
Grandma's 1914 Letter	49
Thomas Reed Covell	53
Thomas Reed Covell	57
Paines	59
George Vasey	61
Tindale-Vasey	63
Vasey Generations	72
Vasey Children	73
Imogene And The Traveling Trunk	75
Heritage	82
Paine Family Record	84
Civil War News	85
Civil War Letter	87
Moms Writing	89
Harold's Story	93
Early Years	98
Cowboy Daddy	108
From My Mother's Bible	109
New Beginnings	110

Going On	112
Remembering	113
Growing Up Country	114
Early Days	116
Ted And Me	119
Feed Sacks	121
Special Christmas	123
Goosecreek Fire	125
Memories Live On	127
Togetherness	131
Looking Back	133
Christmas	135
Country Progress	137
Best Friends	139
Country Living	142
Canoeing	143
Country Cuts	145
Sleepy And A Gun	147
Electricity	149
Country Family	151
Measles	153
The '49 Blizzard	155
Work And Fun	157
Quilts Tie Families	158
Quilts	161
Setting Goals	162
Sewing	165
A Memorable Christmas	167
Water	168
Comfort Food	169
Remedies	171
Little Cowboys	175
Calendar Entries Of Our Five Year Old	177
The Last Cattle Drive	179
Our Pony	181
Blessings	183
Honesty	185
Country Sit-Com	186
Wildfire	189
First Tractor	191
Grandchildren	193
Writing Joys	195
Warming Solution	197
Contests	199

Important	201
Parent Tribute	204
Veterans Day	206
Veterans	207
Iwo Jima Veteran	209
Why?	211
Little Hero	213
Ranch/Farm Tribute	217
My Farmer	220
Wheel Chair Olympics	221
Tribute To John	222
Comparing	226
Women And Peace	228
Suddenly Alone	231
Family Reunion	235
The Gift	237
Red Rose	238
Butterfly	239
My Angels	240
Blank Book	242
London	244
Impressive Sites Visited	246
World Travel	251
Conclusion	254
Sandhills Sunshine	255
Other Family Pictures	257

INTRODUCTION

My devotion several days after being robbed of our family heirlooms, collections and tools was, "Do not store up for yourselves treasures on earth, where moth and rust destroy, and where thieves break in and steal." Matthew 6:19. I really needed the message that day. I am thankful for the grace to know where my real treasure is and where I am going. I have the assurance to believe the Bible no matter what happens.

Since I have no treasures or antiques to pass to my family, I have collected and put together our family stories. These are memories that cannot be stolen. My grandchildren love to hear about the past and since I am their link, I share these stories with love and prayers that they will be accepted for the information, guidance, fun, love and challenges presented. I am grateful to Harold and his parents for the information they shared. My grandparents and parents shared of themselves and our distant ancestors stories. Home is where love flourishes with family, not about possessions or dollars.

Gathering these stories has been a challenging labor of love. It has been an adventure to organize and write, what I hope will be meaningful memories, of the life we lived with divergent hardships, laughter and hope for my family and future generations. We lived through difficult times and happy times all in the country. I trust my efforts will be accepted as I poured much time and effort into writing them. It is my prayer that these stories will prove interesting as well as a witness to the strong character and faith of our remarkable ancestors. I hope these words will remind us of the many blessings as a family living in the grass covered Sandhills and scenic pine clad butte country of Western Nebraska.

Our Mama, Irene, holding baby Ted, with Lila, four years old, Beth, one, and Jim, two, standing close, taken by her good friend Ruby Hansen.

ROBBED!

"You have been robbed! Come quick!" son Wayne urged on the telephone at noon on a damp spring day of 2008. Wayne and Julie had driven past and then backed up, noticing a shop door flopping in the wind. Inspection revealed the house and every out building had been broken into. Doors, locks, windows and latches were broken. The big solid wooden house door had been pushed in by brute force.

I was watching my four year old granddaughter, so we hurriedly headed home after calling the sheriff. Deputy Sheriff Jarvis met us at the gate. Alyssa acted extremely agitated.

Alyssa gripped my hand tightly as we walked through the house with the deputy sheriff inspecting messes, open cupboard doors and drawers. My things strewn everywhere. Alyssa's mom drove from work as soon as possible. She told her mother, when she saw the deputy, "I thought you weren't coming home!" That is when I learned this was the same deputy who had informed her mother that her daddy wasn't coming home, less than a year earlier. She told me, "He is the one who made my Mommy cry." Her daddy had promised he would help me move my shelves, dolls, lamps, pitchers and old dishes on Saturday. Then he was crushed on Friday. The robbery was a sharp reminder of hurting memories for both of us.

My family and I are all upset that people have blatantly taken property that is not theirs. Evidence is strewn everywhere. Mean perpetrators dumped every drawer and opened every cabinet door. A hand embroidered picture made by my mother is gone. My love letters, of 50 years before, from my late husband were scattered and trampled. His pocket knife collection is gone. Old pictures were knocked down and glass broken. Tin type pictures of ancestors were taken. Harold's baby shoes are missing. A huge antique curve topped steamer trunk filled with irreplaceable family heirlooms is gone. Old lamps, dishes and dolls are gone! My class ring and old jewelry pieces are missing. Old quilts, my high school letter sweater, my children's baby shoes, pants, dresses and sweaters are gone.

Great Grandmother Paine lived near Chicago during the Chicago Fire of 1871. A treasure she brought to Nebraska was tiny melted doll dishes. Aunt Maud had the dishes in 1947. Years later I told Aunt Mildred. She said, "I have those dishes; I can send them to you." I was thrilled to have the melted dishes. I told my children and put a note on them stating the year of the fire. I showed my grandchildren and shared the melted dish story. The dishes sat prominently in my cupboard for years until they, and the shelf, were stolen. Many tiny pitchers, a monk bank with "Thou shall not steal" on his front, a decorative dish that said, "He who indulges, bulges" were stolen. A collection of small plates from my mother's cousin, were in my cupboard and are not now. Two large ornate tea pots, trays and delicate cups, given to us by our elderly Danish neighbor, are gone. I was little but I watched Mr. Larsen tearfully wrap the dishes for my mother and me, after his wife's death. He wanted us to have them to cherish and I did. Tiny cup and saucers from a great aunt were taken. A Civil War mug used by nurse Lettie was taken. Six unique very old family kerosene lamps were on a shelf and they vanished that day.

Old plates, spoons, dishes and teapots belonging to my husband's family, and mine, were confiscated. An ancient pewter pipe, an ornate hair bowl and sugar bowl from Gramps' family were in the cupboard but are not now. Gibbons treasurers are gone. A large bowl with a note by Maud Paine said, "1880 Orleans store opening," is gone. Very old calendars and fancy colloid hair combs are gone. The old butter churn, my collections of tea pots, dolls, over 3000 buttons sewn in a book and Grandma's pink glass depression dishes are missing. A gallon jar of old buttons was taken. A valuable doll with a white leather body, porcelain head, hands and feet, and lovely blond curls, a gift to Elsie, my mother's double cousin in 1915, was stolen. My list goes on... and on.

Friends helped move the few items left to my garage. Two weeks later the robbers returned!! They cut my large new padlock, broke open the bolted door and took what was left there then drove to clean out my garage! The chain saw, welder, helmet, air tank, battery charger and tools belonging to my late husband plus the contents of 'my room.' My special doll collection, dolls from friends and family were stolen. A collection of artifacts, arrow heads, Indian beads and a petrified sea shell collected by the Gibbons family, for generations were taken. I learned later the very old ones were worth lots. Gramps had given me some old family jewelry which is missing. The robbers left a mess and nothing of value. There are clues at each location so maybe there is a chance to catch the robbers yet if the Sheriff department will follow through to check. Alyssa prays that the police will find and convict them. Those who took our treasures must live with their guilt and conscience. I can share memories with my family. We will live trying to be better rather than bitter.

Gramps Harry Gibbons' Grandparents, Joseph and Sara Strange Gibbons taken in North Hampton, England before they came to America.

ANCESTORS

FAMILY

When I was looking for a class for college credits a number of years ago to renew my teaching certificate, I called a professor listed beside a genealogy class. I asked questions about the class. He informed me, "Most people do not know the names of grandparents and rarely great grandparents." I was surprised, I actually knew my great grandmother and had heard stories of many other ancestors. I asked my father-in-law for his grandparents' names. It took him, and his brother Roy, both past 85, awhile but they came up with names of their grandmother and grandfather. I decided the genealogy class was not what I needed. My great aunts recorded our family ancestry back for generations as a pastime. Their nephew did research in a library in the east. Names, dates and stories were recorded for future family members. I wrote a generation chart for my family to visualize how far back some records take us with names and birth dates. I updated Jerry and Wayne's so this is current to 2011.

GENERATIONS OF FAMILY

13TH Century Baron Johannen Von Haight—Normandy and Britain

1595 Simon Haight—Dorsetshire, England

1620 Nicholas Hoit—Salem, Massachusetts Colony, married Susannah Joyce

1649 Johnathan Hoit married Mary Bell, daughter of Francis Bell

1683 Johnathan Hoit married Martha Dudley, daughter of Johnathan Dudley

1754 Judge Jonathan Hoit married Lois Bradley, daughter of Joseph Bradley

1788 Heman Hoit married Susan Franklin, daughter of Oliver and Cynthia Pratt

1817 Mary Orton Hoit married Dr. Fulwar Skipwith Paine, son of Seth Paine and

1845 Cassius Paine married Cornelia Covell daughter of Thomas and Elizabeth Brown Covell

1881 Claude Paine married Henrietta Vasey daughter of George and Margaret Tindale Vasey

1909 Irene Paine married Paul Weber son of William and Maude Burris Weber

1937 Elizabeth Weber married Harold Gibbons son of Harry and Gertrude Crowell Gibbons

***

1960 Jerry Gibbons married Kathy Serres daughter of Ernest and Alice Serres

1985 Andrew Gibbons married Cassandra Dawn Koch daughter of

2008 Joseph Gibbons and 2009 Addie Nichole Gibbons

***

1962 Wayne Gibbons married Julie Toof daughter of Donald and Evelyn Toof

1987 Cody Gibbons married Tonya Housh daughter of Gary and Bonnie Housh

2007 Carson Wayne Gibbons and 2011 Treye Rueger Gibbons

GIBBONS FAMILY
Quotes from Harry Gibbons 1970

"The Gibbons trace ancestors to Thomas and Jennie Gibbons. She was born November 23, 1770 in England. Grandfather, Joseph Gibbons, their son, was born in North Hampton, England on March 25, 1835. He worked in a gun factory in Illion, Illinois making rifle barrels for the Remington Arms Company foundry during the Civil War for the war effort. He was later a blacksmith in Waterloo, Nebraska. I saw a solid lot covered with walking plows waiting for him to sharpen. Grandmother, Sarah (Strange) Gibbons, was born in Mohawk, New York. Her ancestors were from En gland. She had a tin type picture of her father. They moved to Elkhorn, Nebraska in 1882. He died at home in Waterloo on June 1, after retiring two years earlier.

"My father, William Henry Gibbons was born in Utica, New York in 1860. Mother, Fannie Elizabeth (Bryant) Gibbons was born on December 16,1866 in Elk City, Nebraska. Her father was an old settler in Nebraska. Mother told about the Indians looking in their windows begging for bread. As a young girl she saw her parents give bread to the Indians, hoping they would go away. Their home was a little log house that, years later, was covered with siding. Roy, Clara and I climbed the stairs to their attic looking at the old rifles—musket loaders.

"Mother's father was out looking for hogs that got out and ran through the timber. He was a short heavyset fellow and caught pneumonia, dying the next day. Her parents had a cider mill in their shop and we kids ran apples through the press for fresh cider juice. They had a big orchard so we gathered many apples. We kids crushed apples for good fresh apple juice. My folks were farmers near Florence, Nebraska. When we were young, Roy and I walked along the Missouri River looking for the steamboat, "The Bertrand" that sank around 1860. It was discovered a few miles north of our home in 1969. We frequently found arrow heads on the farm ground near the river's edge.

"Joe Hipp, Roy and I, spent time near the river when we weren't doing chores. Joe, who died in 1970, came walking over the hill every day. Steam boats were seldom seen on the river; we fished all day without disturbance. We spent one Sunday afternoon getting a steamboat off a sand bar. The men rocked and dug around the boat to move it into deep water.

"Roy stepped on a blood snake which bit him on the ankle. He ran home and doctored it but it took a long time to heal. (He showed the still visible scar at 1988.) Roy, Clara and I walked three miles to the Gary Owen School, between Fort Calhoun and our home. One morning when I was eight and Clara, six, we were walking to school when three big gray timber wolves walked out on the road. The folks made us ride to school in a two wheeled cart pulled by a horse after that. We put hay and an ear of corn or two in a sack for the horse.

"One 4th of July, my dad and the neighbors went for a sail boat ride up the Missouri River. The wind came up and tipped the boat over. One man swam out but Dad and the other man hung on drifting for five miles until they were picked up at Florence. I had gone to the neighbors to take care of their livestock and when I came back I found the picnic abandoned. There was a cat on the table. The women and children were down by the river watching the men float down the river. The men had tied the gale rope tight instead of controlling the boat with it like they should have. They finally brought in a large boat to save the men. Our family used the big boat for years to go hunting and fishing along the river.

"I attended Walthill High School where many half and quarter breed Native American Indians attended. The girls were very pretty. We students went to ball games when Walter Hamilton, later known as Chief Spotted Back, was playing on our town team. He was one of the best players for the Walthill Indians. Whites and Indians played together on the team. We attended the Omaha Indians' Pow Wow every year at harvest time. Other tribes came from near and as far away as Oklahoma to dance. The Winnebago tribe was just north of there; they would dance all day. They gave calico dress goods and sometimes a horse to their friends. They gathered in the big tent and called a name and give gifts. Then they would sing and dance some more. A carnival was on the grounds with a merry-go-around and often a ball game. Many Indians camped in tents in rows as long as a city street. We had a good Indian neighbor, Charley Pilcher, who stacked straw for us when we threshed. Charlie was a relative of Chief Spotted Back who traveled to England and to Crawford on the train with a group of Omaha boy scouts.

"A picture of me at 16, in 1906, was taken at Clyde Deyos place when I helped him carry baskets of grapes to Omaha for the open market. We got up at three in the morning to pack fruit for early market. Mr. Deyo put baskets together and sold them for 15 cents each.

"Land agent Arah Hungerford from Crawford, advertised, 'Let me help you get a farm in the "Garden Beyond the Sandhills".' The ad interested my parents. They came out on the train to look at the property. They signed the papers on October 22, 1910. Father moved in early January 1911. We were ready to come when Roy, Clara and I broke out with the measles. We had to wait a week as we were really sick. Father came with his cows, horses and machinery by train. I attended York Business College during the spring sessions in 1912, 1913 and 1914, graduating with a Commercial Business degree. I raised corn to make enough money to pay for my tuition and college expenses. (I asked if he was going to York to see his high school sweetheart. He smiled mischievously but did not deny the idea.)

"In 1918, I got my first car, a dark blue Maxwell. The first trip I drove the Maxwell to the Rex Tollman place for a picnic. We didn't need driver's licenses but had to take along a shovel. I got stuck on high center before getting home. The car was handy for courting and going to parties. Before that we traveled with a team and buggy. Once old Dolly ran into a tree and tore up her harness. We went to church on the corner by our place and tied our horses to a hitching rail. One Sunday we found the single tree, or neck yoke, was tangled and broke.

"Gertie and I courted by mail and were married on January 1, 1920 in her parent's home. She chose her brother Vyrle and sister Eva as our attendants. After a big family meal we caught the train headed to Omaha where we visited aunts and uncles: Mr. And Mrs. Len Fitch, Mr. and Mrs. H.K. Mansfield, my mother's sisters and families. Returning to Walthill, we packed our belongings and loaded her big piano on the train headed for Crawford. We went west visiting in Waterloo; Lena and Charles Killett and Uncle Joe and Aunt Mary Gibbons in Elk Horn and in Wood Lake, Mr. and Mrs. Oscar Kelly and their family. We settled on a small rented farm south-east of Crawford for 20 years, next to my parents, where Harold was born. I rode to town for the doctor when he arrived. Her mother came out on the train to help while he was tiny. Gertie was in bed for two weeks. That was the way they did then. Harold rode his horse to attend school District #25. He stayed in an apartment one semester then drove or rode to high school with the Williams brothers, Gordon, Ivan, Gerald and Royce.

"Soldiers of the 12th Cavalry drill team from Fort Robinson came to Crawford to celebrate the 4th of July. The fort brought their equestrian team and put on quite a show. They jumped singly and in pairs over hurdles on the race track. There was a filling station where Knapp's Store was. The livery barn was on the corner where the Post Office is. A Livery Stable was down the street where John Deere Implement is. We drove to see livery when it caught fire.

"Indians danced in streets of dirt in Crawford between the bank and Murphy store. They wore little leather loin cloths and bright feathers. Hundreds danced at fair time and on the 4th of July. We'd drive in with a horse and buggy to watch and later in the Maxwell car."

(Robert Walker, son of Harry's cousin, Mary Ann Gibbons Walker, wrote, "One story I remember about my Great Granddad Gibbons, was that his parents wanted to leave Nebraska because they were afraid of Indians. They went to Monet, Missouri where a blacksmith was needed. That's where my Great Grandfather, Fred Gibbons lost his father. A railroad detective came in his blacksmith store to buy ammunition for his pistol. He was loading the pistol with his back to my great grandfather. The gun misfired and struck a pot bellied stove and ricocheted back hitting him in the stomach. He died three days later. My granddad, who I knew as Gramps, had to quit school to support his mother and sisters when he was 11. He went to work for the railroad and finally retired when he was 70." *John and Kristi met Robert and Trish Walker when they took a college business trip in 1995. They visited them in their home.

*Harry was 70 when he became a grandfather for the first time, a role he thoroughly enjoyed. Jerry began calling him Gramps and he loved his new title. He was a wonderful grandpa to Jerry, Wayne and Kristi, who he thought were extra special. Harry lived to be 94, driving his 1948 Chevrolet car until he was 92. When the insurance agent said his car insurance was due, Gramps replied, "It's all right I will just drive around town." The agent was upset and called us to report his response. Gramps told us he wasn't going to drive anymore. He realized he had hit the side of his garage and wasn't handling his car so good.

Gibbons grandchildren still quote Gramps and reminisce of good times spent with him and Grandma Gibbons. They remember his vast knowledge of weather and country life and her good cooking and immaculate housekeeping. Their life was an example of good. He grew a big garden and raised beautiful flowers which they shared. They were greatly loved by their family. Gramps told me he would give up all his utilities before his telephone. That is when we realized how important our daily phone calls to him were. It is humbling and gratifying.

Gramps, Harry Gibbons, standing beside his 1918 Maxwell car which he donated for the WWII scrap drive in 1943.

GRAMPS' WEATHER PROGNOSTICATIONS

"Remember 2010's rainy season and the weeks since Easter?" Son Jerry reminded me of Gramps' quote, "If it rains on Easter there will be seven weeks of rain." It rained on Easter and we had a very wet spring. Gramps was a weather prognosticator and we listened to his worthy weather adages. I talked to him every day during his last ten years, while widowed and living alone. I wrote his predictions on the flip side of my calendars as I wanted to draw on his wisdom to record the many sayings. My calendars have vanished but his wisdom remains with his grandchildren for which I am grateful.

Forecasts for good weather abound. Listen to birds singing as confirmation of good days. Smoke rises when good weather is coming. A barometer will be down when chimney smoke goes down to the ground. Animals and children running and playing noisily means a storm is coming. My mother said, "There must be a storm brewing," when we were being overly rowdy. Gramps and his son heard a 'rain crow' and announced, "It is going to rain." I watched, observing, and it rained in a day or two.

Weather adages Gramps quoted were: Red sails at night sailor's delight; red sails in the morning sailors take warning. A fuzzy caterpillar is a sign of a hard winter. A sun dog (small rainbow) around the sun in the winter means a storm is coming. It will rain if earth worms come to ground surface. Two frosts and lots of rain mean that the cold season is near. The weather will be bad in winter if you see hornets and yellow jackets building nests solid and closer to the ground. A lot of spiders and black bugs in the fall means a hard winter. Ants build their hill higher or ant covering their hole indicates it will soon rain. Loud train noises are signs of low barometer and changing weather. Country people working the land plan their work based on watching and observing weather conditions. I am glad my sons and daughter recall quotes from Gramps. Nothing keeps memories alive like sharing and remembering Gramp's wisdom.

GREAT GRANDFATHER BRYANT

Harold's Great Grandfather John Bryant and his brother Joe arrived in the United states in 1855 from England. They, with their trusty single shot rifles, traveled on foot across the wide open country from the east coast to Chicago and later on to Nebraska.

The Bryant brothers built a cabin from local wood shaping the boards and shingles with their tools. A two story cabin was built for their new home in eastern Nebraska.

One night they returned from town where they had gone shopping for groceries and supplies. Listening, they heard a soft pit-a-pat sound coming from within their home. They then noticed an open window and soon closed it.

Going inside, they lit a candle and cautiously looked around. Up on the stairs a pair of yellow eyes glowed in the candle light, reflecting back at them.

Quickly, the animal turned and softly padded higher on the stairs. Great Grandfather Bryant grabbed his single shot gun and pulled the trigger. A large wild cat fell dead, dropping down the stairs to land at his feet.

Ever after, any questions about holes in the side of the house brought a retelling of the story of a big wildcat that came calling when no one was home. The grandparents kept that board with the holes when they moved.

Harry 'Gramps' Gibbons often repeated this story about his Grandfather John Bryant to Harold and I and to Jerry, Wayne and Kristi. He had seen the cutout piece of wood with bullet holes in it. Later I found a newspaper copy of the story written by a young descendant of Joe Bryant which added other details of the story. The protective need of a gun was effectively demonstrated. We never tired of hearing him repeat the details of this story.

W. H. GIBBONS

Great Grandfather William Henry Gibbons, son of blacksmith, Joseph and his wife Sarah (Strange) Gibbons, came to Crawford from Florence, Nebraska on a steam train with all their possessions in early 1911. William's wife, Fannie Elizabeth (Bryant) Gibbons came later with their children, Roy, Harry and Clara. The W. H. Gibbons purchased a farm property near Crawford from Sara DeGraff, sold by land agent Arah Hungerford who originated and often promoted the area with the still used slogan, "The Garden Beyond the Sandhills."

William Roy Gibbons, known as Roy, was born near Elk City on January 13, 1888, the day the infamous blizzard began. Gramps told us his father rode his horse to a neighbors for a midwife for Roy's birth. Uncle Roy married Rosella Thornton of Crawford. They were parents of Gertrude and Wanda who married the Douthit brothers. Gertrude and Donald moved to Idaho and raised six children: Donna Jean Ash, Marilyn Blattner, Shirley Wadsworth, Gerald, Roger (Bill) and Daniel. Wanda and Dale lived in Whitney and Crawford having Melvin, Norma Cozad, Lonnie, and twins: Gayle Stetson and Galen. Clara married Frank Soester and they had, Hazel, Wilbur and Alice, before moving to Harlingen, Texas.

Harry, born May 20, 1890, at Elk City, graduated from Walt Hill High school and York Business College. On January 1, 1920, he returned to Walthill to marry his high school sweetheart Gertrude Isabell Crowell at her parents home, Walter and Alice Irene Crowell. Harry and Gertie were parents of Harold Don born at home on December 12, 1923 near Crawford just south of his Grandparent's. Harold rode his horse to District #25 school through the 8th grade. He graduated from Crawford High School in 1941. After the death of his grandmother Fannie Elizabeth Gibbons, Harry and Gertie moved in with Granddad, W. H. Gibbons, to care for him in his later years. They bought the farm shares from his siblings Roy and Clara and celebrated 50 years together in January 1970. Gertie lived to be 81 and Harry 94 years. They shared much wisdom and love with their three much loved grandchildren.

Harold married Beth on May 24, 1959 in the Chadron Baptist Church. They became parents of Jerry Dean, Wayne Harold and Kristi Irene. Harold worked hard on the family farm all his life. One winter before his marriage, he helped Frank Anderson sell cars and deliver cars from Denver. He said he learned a lot about people that winter. Harold liked most to see plants and animals grow. He suffered a sudden fatal heart attack on May 18, 1992. Beth still lives and works on the Gibbons family farm plus she does substitute teaching and writing. Harold and Beth shared love with their children and grandchildren. They took them along with them whenever possible to the field, to get animal feed or to town. Our biggest thrill was sharing time with these little ones. Only Andy and Will were old enough to remember Harold, their grandpa. Andy said, "Grandpa always said, 'I was a good boy' so I will be a good boy." I trust Andy will remember, continue to be a good guy and to share special memories of his Grandpa Harold with his brothers, sisters and cousins.

Jerry married Kathy Lanell Serres on January 2, 1983 in the Chadron Baptist Church. He manages Charter Cable Television Company in the panhandle and as far east as Kearney. Kathy sells Modern Woodman Insurance and works at the Scottsbluff Hospital. They are parents of Andrew Paul who graduated from Hemingford High School and Mitchel South Dakota Technical College. He married Cassandra Dawn Koch in Joy, Illinois on June 15, 2003. Andy and Dawn have Joseph Ronald born October 31, 2007 and Addie Nichole, born February 27, 2009. William Scott broke his neck in a car roll over accident in September 2002 and graduated from Hemingford High School in 2005. He sells insurance. Joseph Dean was born July 19, 1988 and died of a malignant brain stem tumor, October 31, 1999, at 11 years. Jerry and Kathy adopted Mindra Oana Lynda and Ana Angelica of Romania and Ben Romel and Ivan John from Russia. They adopted Maria Grace of Donetsk, Estonia and Jade SuSu of China. The children attend school in Hemingford. Marina, cried to belong to a family, at 16 when she was adopted; the orphanage was ready to oust her. Marina married Lyman Aguallo on December 30, 2010 and they live happily in Scottsbluff where Lyman works for Cable Television. Mindy graduated with honors May 8, 2011 from Hemingford High School.

She plans to attend Chadron State College to study music and business.

Wayne and Julie Ann Toof were married January 1, 1986 in Hay Springs Methodist Church. They are parents of Cody Don born July 12, 1987 and Ashley Elizabeth born January 21, 1992. Both graduated from Crawford High School. Cody married Tonya Kae Housh of Hay Springs, on March 19, 2006 in Fort Lewis, Washington, so she could get her passport to Germany. They had a family and friends wedding, outside where they met at Fort Robinson on June 16, 2006. They are parents of Carson Wayne born March 5, 2007 in Germany and Treye Rueger born March 10, 2011 in Alliance. Sgt Cody served in the Army in Iraq and Germany. He is in the National Guard attending Chadron State College where he made the Dean's honor roll. He gave the Silver Dollar First Salute to a graduate during ceremonies spring 2011. Ashley, an honor student, was a HOBY scholar and Internet voice of the Rams. She attends college at Riverton, Wyoming studying art and photography. Wayne raises honey bees producing and selling barrels of honey. Julie sews, makes candles, lotions, salves and flavored honey from honey products.

Kristi married John Timothy Snyder, of Rapid City, South Dakota, on December 28, 1996 in Crawford. Kristi and John were parents of Gabriel, still-born in 2001 and daughter Alyssa Mae born September 11, 2003. John died in a tragic accident May 11, 2007. Kristi and Alyssa live near Chadron. Kristi is an AFLAC insurance agent in South Dakota and Nebraska. Alyssa will attend Chadron City Schools because all rural schools closed in May 2011.

The Gibbons are still friends with the DeGraff and Hipp-Graves descendants generations later. We celebrated 100 years of Gibbons family ownership in 2010 with recognition at the Dawes County Fair grounds by AKSARBEN and the Dawes County Fair.

AUNT CINA

By Hannah Crowell Rogers

Lucinda Crowell was born October 25, 1860 in Sun Prairie County, Wisconsin and died June 7, 1888. She was raised in Decatur, Nebraska, the only daughter of Elisha and Polly (Stiles) Crowell. She was a sister to Walter Crowell. (My children's great great grandfather.)

Cina was admired and adored by everyone among her family, relatives and friends. In young womanhood she became efficient in sewing, especially dressmaking. She drafted her own patterns and they fit. Pattern drafting was done by taking measurements and cutting according to the measurements.

Cina established a dressmaker's shop in Lyons, Nebraska, where she was successfully self-employed for a time. She was courted and engaged to marry a young man named George Hart, son of an early pioneer. For some reason they separated and several years later she married Edward Biggs. They had a happy marriage spending their first year on a cattle ranch owned by Tim Carbine (or Carbien) near Emerson, Nebraska as ranch hand and cook. Carbine owned a larger ranch nearby. Grandpa Elisha Crowell worked on the bigger ranch.

Aunt Cina and Uncle Ed's friends, Mr. and Mrs. Joseph Kurtz of Bancroft, Nebraska had gone to Helena, Montana to cook for men working in the Green Valley Gold Mine about four miles from Helena. The couples' corresponded telling of doing well, enjoying their work and making new friends. It was suggested this would be a good adventure for Cina and Ed and there was much discussion among the relatives. Most tried to discourage them.

Cina and Ed went by train to Helena, stopping first in Omaha to visit friends, nieces of George Hart. As they had postponed buying a wedding ring, the friends, Linnie and Lela Hart helped her choose a wedding ring. After working at Helena awhile Ed and Cina heard of Maiden Mine in Wyoming and decided to try working there. They traveled by covered wagon.

The couple met a man walking and invited him to ride with them as he was heading to the same place. People who had met them along the way marveled that this stranger was shooting at birds and anything else along the way. Later they supposed he was getting the horses used to his shooting.

The couples were to reach their destination the following noon but that was not to be. The man they had taken in and trusted with their only means of protection shot and killed them with their own weapons in their wagon that night. Four grown people and Ida Schans, a six year old girl the Kurtz were caring for, at her father's request, after her mother died at the mining camp, were all dead. There was no sign of violence on the little girl. Authorities believe she was drowned where they intended to camp that night.

This was one of the brutal tragedies of the early West. The tragedy seemed so very unbelievable to people in Helena and Wyoming. The news aroused cowboys who were soon on the trail of the murderer and put him in jail. The murderer had been in trouble before and knew what would happen so to escape he hanged himself in his cell with strips of bed blankets. Indications were that James Wilber, alias Henry Patterson, deliberately shot these people and drew a cover over their bodies and drove thirty-five miles to the Judith River where he disposed of them.

Cowboys discovered Mrs. Kurtz' body when their cattle stampeded and ran to the river. They buried her, as an unknown by the river, then discovered the other four and remembered seeing them traveling in the vicinity. News of their identity soon got around. All were buried by the river but later were moved to a cemetery in Lewiston, Montana. The murderer, Wilber or Patterson, had driven their team and covered wagon to a ranch and traded for another, then somewhere had gotten a peddler's outfit. He was traveling through the country as a peddler when captured. He had, among his jewelry, the wedding ring bought for Aunt Cina in Omaha. Her Omaha friends identified the ring because they had been with her when it was purchased. The other jewelry was peddler quality. There is no doubt a crime was committed with intent of robbery. He may have obtained a lot of money, which was deposited in a bank in Helena before leaving. Clothing was brought back to positively identify Aunt Cina and Uncle Ed.

This is the way I heard this story over and over, from the time I was eleven years old, until time healed the wound. Dedicated to the family and descendants of the Elisha Crowell Clan. Signed Hannah Crowell Rogers, age 85, September 15, 1962.

(This family history from Gertrude Crowell Gibbons, was written by her cousin, Hannah Lucinda Crowell Rogers who wrote details of Aunt Cina as she heard them in 1888 and after.)

CROWELL ANCESTORS

Ancestors recorded stories are for us to learn from and appreciate. I copied records from, "Early Settlers in Eastern Burt County" written by Hannah Lucinda Rogers, born September 15, 1877. The booklet records Crowell ancestors back to Great Grandfather Edward Crowell born August 16, 1794, 'somewhere in England' and his wife was Alpha Dickinson Crowell born September 30, 1795 in England.

"Hannah wrote, "The Crowells were sea faring people. Their son, Elisha Crowell, born March 12, 1821, married Polly Bracket Stiles who was born February 23 1823. Her parents were Otis Baker and Harriet Wareham Stiles Baker. Harriet's parents were Wareham and Melinda More Stiles born in Massachusetts. Edward Crowells' written will gave $5 to each of his children and a grandson, 'to be paid-severely-one year from my death.'"

Captain Crowell had a ship which fell victim to pirates when French pirates were roving rampant all along the Barbary Coast. A large sum of money was paid to the United States by the French Government in restoration for the robberies of ships and their cargoes on the high seas. It was called, "The French Spoliation Claim." Many families were entitled to payments for robberies of ships belonging to their ancestors. Some may have been successful in collecting dollars but not the Crowell family of our ancestry. Congress canceled the claims.

Polly Bracket Stiles' Uncle, Charles L. Anthony was a cousin to Susan B. Anthony, the first woman to make a speech starting the Women's Suffrage Movement. Elisha and Polly Crowell traveled by covered wagon with their family and other families from West Hawley, Massachusetts to Wisconsin and over the Missouri River to Tieville, Iowa, across from Decatur. Later Elisha Crowell bought the saw mill and flat boat ferry from Robert Moore. They called their ferry, "The Queen of Decatur."

Early church services were held in school houses and called, "Going to meeting." All the neighbors went to meetings. The Crowell family loaned their organ for traveling entertainers and therefore were permitted to attend for free. Parades included many soldiers, children dressed up and Indians riding their ponies in costumes—headdress, beaded moccasins, tomahawks and leggings. Native Americans wore trophies of eagle feathers, squirrel tails, bear claws and teeth. Now and then there was a white man's scalp. Indian dances, songs, speeches, give aways and ball games or horse races followed the July 4th parades.

Walter and Alice Irene Crowell at Lyons, Nebraska with their first three daughters, Eva, Clara and Baby Gertie in 1892.

GRANDMA GIBBONS

Gertrude Isabell Crowell Gibbons, the third of six children, was born to Walter and Alice Irene Crowell at Lyons, Nebraska on June 21, 1892. She was about five foot one inches tall and had red hair and blue eyes. She enjoyed telling about her little brother Vyrle singing for family and strangers as a tiny tot. She said a grocer put him on the counter and he sang there too. Gertie attended elementary school at Lyons and high school at Walthill and then worked at the U.S. Post Office at Walthill, Pender and Wakefield, Nebraska and Sioux City, Iowa. She was united in marriage to Harry Arthur Gibbons at Walthill.

Gertie said when she was little the local ministers played their piano and others gave lessons using it. She liked to play the piano and belonged to the Crow Butte Extension Club for many years. She looked forward to attending club and visiting with the members every month.

The couple celebrated 50 years together in Crawford with an open house in their honor in January 1970. They delighted in their grandsons Jerry and Wayne who helped decorate the church for the celebration. Beth and Margaret Zimmerman decorated their anniversary cake. Gertie passed away on Friday evening, January 18, 1974, in the Chadron Hospital. She was proceeded in death by her sisters Eva, a WWI nurse who served in France and was an artist and a school nurse in Wala Wala, Washington, and Clara, a teacher who contacted the 1919 flu. She often referred to "We little girls." Her younger sister Deanna Crowell, a long time Sioux City, Iowa, teacher living at Fort Dodge, Iowa and brothers Ralph, a former farmer living at Oakland and Vyrle, a business man, in Rosalie, survived her.

DAD'S MEMORIES

as told to Beth on January 26, 1995

Dad began sharing his memories shortly before he died when I took notes: "The old house where I was born was in a grove of trees, east of the present home. The outside door opened to nothing. I went over and tore the house down. I hauled the lumber home with team and wagon. I drove the Model T to Ainsworth to bring Mom and the baby twins, Flora and Florence, home from the hospital, in March 1931. One rode on the back window and one was held on Mom's lap. There wasn't room for her to hold both babies. I was 24 and there had been a snow storm so we came through deep drifts.

"Your mother and I got married on May 6, 1933. Irene was teaching a country school; she had a week of school left. Jelinek and others came to shivery us. Mildred was little and wanted to go wherever we went. My sisters were all born after I was grown. I don't remember living at home when I had sisters. Myrle was born June 1923, by then I was away working. I worked for Harry Keller where I got my start raising Hereford cattle; I was paid with livestock.

"I picked corn for three cents a bushel for Otto Sclintz and for Bauers in Logan County. The first year I went down there afoot. Cousin John Weber brought me home. I bought a 1929 Model A the next year from Chester Fink on time payments. He sold the most cars of anyone in the state at that time. He sold Dad a 1918 Model T. Chester Fink built a garage to service the cars he sold in the country around Elsmere.

"In 1931, Etta, Claude and Mildred Paine were given a ride with Benson from Texas to invest in land. They paid all their cow money, $20 a head, and lost it all in the down payment. There wasn't enough money for more payments."

(Dad didn't often share stories of difficulties of hard work but good times with family. He joined neighbors to help brand. He roped and held calves or wielded the branding irons or knife. He felt badly when he was asked to man the gates, which was considered a safer job.

His folks married September 15, 1906. Dad was born August 6, 1907 in their sod house on the prairie a few miles east of where he spent his life. His mother said his first bed was her sewing machine top. Her Aunt Minnie, a teacher, had a homestead that joined theirs. They lived hours from neighbors or a town A mail carrier came every other day— when roads were so he could. There was no phone, running water or electricity for years—until the fall of 1953.

Dad was mowing prairie hay, as a five year old, tied on the seat of a horse pulled mower. He grew strong and responsible. The Weber family attended Sunday School in the rural school house going in a horse pulled wagon, as did their neighbors.

For the ninth grade, Dad rode his horse to a neighboring school traveling nine miles each way. He worked at a hotel to pay for his board and room to attend high school in Thedford as a 10th grader. He said he cut fresh bread for the hotel to serve customers. He several times demonstrated how to turn the loaf and cut properly with a serrated knife.

Dad went outside to feed his dog, Lucky, at Ahrens the evening of August 5, 1996 and fell with a heart attack. He had attended the Dawes County Fair with Cody, nine, Ashley, four, and me. He enjoyed watching Cody announced as the Junior 4-H Showmanship Champion. Dad had just taken a new prescription medicine. We were all thankful he didn't fall while he was home alone—50 miles from any doctor. He was with family and enjoyed his last day.

We loved and respected our Dad and Mother. She died two years earlier and Dad grieved for her every day from then on. In August 2007, my siblings and I met to celebrate our dad and mother on what would have been Dad's 100th birthday. We sorted and divided pictures, sharing stories of good times and tears, reminiscing about our family and neighbors in the Sandhills - heritage of stories worth sharing.

W. W. WEBER

Living in the early years of our country was a unique experience. Children grew up fast and accepted great responsibilities at an early age. Our ancestors were no exception. They earned the respect of all who knew them and took on responsibilities at a very young age.

Granddaddy William Weber was born in Esslingen, Germany, May 20, 1877, near Stuttgart. He traveled to America in 1879, on a ship along with many other immigrants, his parents, brothers and sisters. In the old country our name was Weaver, we understood, but officials did not understand the accent and wrote 'Weber.' I visited with people from Germany and asked about the Weber name. They said, "Ves, the Vever name is still common." Sounds like it's still anyone's guess.

Grandma Weber said Granddaddy's mother told her, William, a fair, blue eyed, blond, was the darling of the sailing crew. He was trying to walk on the boat during rough waters and was rescued often when water splashed on deck. This lively two year old slipped on the soaked deck so his mother told of their journey with amused concern.

The family came to America leaving a young sister in Germany. "We never knew why she was left behind," my Dad said. He knew his grandfather, Christoph F. Weber regularly sent checks to the old country. He later decided the sister in Germany was receiving medical help and unable to make the long treacherous journey on rough waters to America.

My father's cousin, Caroline Schlintz Clarke, visited Germany years later and got a copy of the Weber family records which she shared. Many babies born in Germany died as infants. Some names were repeated when the original baby died. Four sets of twins and fifteen births were recorded. In birth order our Granddaddy was next to last on the list. The family registered but this was before Ellis Island kept immigrant records. Their last baby, Christopher was born in America and moved out west to live.

Christoph and Jacobina Mack Weber traveled by rail as far as possible then bought a covered wagon to their destination in rural Illinois. Later they traveled by railroad on to Nebraska. William was assigned to ride with the cattle and to keep their herd fed and watered. Finally, they moved by covered wagon to settle in a new land Nebraska. They bought land near Gandy. Weber relatives, generations later, still live in the area.

Granddaddy worked a number of years for William F. Cody, 'Buffalo Bill,' in North Platte when he was young. He told his family all the helpers were fired after Bill was out late at night 'celebrating.' Cody's patient wife told them go to the bunk house and report for work the next morning. Morning came and Bill forgot about firing his helpers so they continued working.

Next, Granddaddy took a job in the gold mine in Lead. He helped mine for gold using pick axes. Employers didn't trust the workers so stripped them and made a through check of each one daily before they left the mine. When a train car rolled over Granddaddy's big toe, he decided this was not a safe operation to work worth miles of isolation from his family. He was working there when his father died and he rode his horse to attend the services. He arrived as his family was leaving the cemetery.

William worked as a ranch hand for the Chappel family near the tiny town of Elsmere, Nebraska. He was sent on horseback late at night to bring a midwife when their daughter Eunice was born. Eunice Chappel grew up and married Roy Burris, William's wife Maude's youngest brother. They lived near Basin, Wyoming and had one son Jimmy.

William, 27, began courting Maude Burris who was taking care of her younger siblings, sending them to country school, while her mother taught school near Valentine. Maude was much younger but she fell for the handsome blue-eyed man. They rode in his horse drawn buggy to Wood Lake to get a train ride to Valentine to get married October 15, 1906. Her mother signed their license as a witness. Maude and William became parents of ten children. Their son Lewis, 13, drowned at home in 1924. Infants Samuel and Pauline lived only days.

Paul, the oldest, was a hard worker who attended Cherry County rural school #102, with his brothers for eight years. He rode his horse to the neighboring school for nine months learning from teacher, Ted Higgins, for 9th grade. For 10th grade he boarded with widow Emma Keller and her family, working at a hotel to earn enough to pay for his room and board. Paul helped at home and for widow Keller earning cattle as pay.

Roy attended high school graduating in Wyoming. He married Bridget who he met while stationed in the Army in Ireland. They moved to Missouri and were parents of five children, Roy Jr, John, William, Linda and Donna.

Lawrence started high school in Ainsworth but graduated in Wyoming. Lawrence met and married Ann while a Navy airplane mechanic in Michigan. They had daughters, Barbara Ann and June Florence and sons David and John.

Chester rode horseback to a rural sod high school south of Ainsworth, for ninth grade staying with our parents, Paul and Irene. He changed to Gandy to graduate from Logan County High School in 1941. He said, "That was a long long cold ride to the sod school in bad weather." Chester married Frieda and they lived in Lincoln after Wyoming. Their family is: Linda Jean, Wanda Jo, Rieda Rae and Jeffery Lynn.

Myrle boarded for high school to graduate from Ainsworth. She married Ralph Lewis of Ainsworth while he was in the Army. They settled at Rocca and later Lincoln. They had Marie Joann, Dorothy Jean, Deanna Beth and Bobby Dean who live in the Lincoln area.

Twins, Flora and Florence graduated from Gandy High in 1949. Florence married Alvin Joy and they had LaVonne, Melvin and Sharon. Sharon is retired from the military service.

Flora married Leslie Snow, who retired after serving many years in the Air Force in California and Alaska. They settled in Montgomery, Alabama and are parents of Larry, Debbie and Bradley Wayne and grandparents of Rhiannon Kelly Bowman.

William and Maude Weber planted large gardens. They raised cattle, horses, chickens and honey bees extracting honey to sell on the mail route to the grocery store in Wood Lake and to others by quart, gallon or five gallons. They put on coveralls, gloves and bee bonnets taking bee smokers to work the bees in the hives. They operated an extractor to get honey from the combs. My Dad raised honey bees for years. I remember helping Dad and our Grandparents cut off wax, extract, fill and weigh jars and five gallon cans of honey.

Granddaddy and Grandma Weber moved to Gandy for Flora and Florence's final high school year. Later they bought a house in Arnold where they were when doctors diagnosed Granddaddy with stomach cancer. He died in the North Platte hospital on October 30, 1953 at age 77. He reached out his hand and shook mine, cheerfully saying, "Howdy, Howdy" when I visited him the last time in the hospital under an oxygen tent. He was always glad to see his grandchildren. The William Weber's celebrated 46 years together.

GRANDMA WEBER

Grandma, Maude Louellen Burris was born at Bagley, Iowa on December 15, 1890. She lived a long active life until March 6, 1990. Her parents were Elizabeth Kathryn Lewellen Burris and William Stacey Burris. She was the oldest of four children. Her sister, Florence Palmer was born January 18, 1893 and died August 24, 1914, burial in the Purdum cemetery. Her brother, Ralph Waldo Burris was born September 7, 1895 and died December 21, 1968 in Canada. Roy Stanton Burris was born April 13, 1899 and died in 1989 in Wyoming. They were admirable men with families who enjoyed visiting their Sandhill relatives and friends. Our family visited Uncle Roy and Aunt Eunice and their son Jimmy in Worland, Wyoming once.

Family legend says a Burris ancestor, Levi Coffin, was president of the Underground Railroad. William Burris's sister, Hattie Hainsworth, wrote young Maude encouraging letters. I read, "Remember you are descendants of royalty." I don't know that story but I sometimes wonder.

When Maude was eight years old her parents divorced. The children were sent to foster homes or stayed with relatives and/or strangers. Maude was unhappy in the orphanage. She said that is when her education ended. She wrote long letters to her family and was still writing past her 90th year. We knew Grandmother was divorced but it was rarely talked about. I was out of high school when my dad told me.

Great Grandmother Elizabeth worked at various jobs while caring for her family. The Kincaid Act enabled Great Grandmother Elizabeth and her sister, 'Minnie' to homestead side by side on a small tract of land in Cherry County. They came by train and left all their luggage and possessions in the Halsey depot. That night the depot burned. Their possessions were all lost in the fire. Elizabeth sent for her children when Maude was about fourteen.

Maude met William W. Weber and they and married in Valentine on October 15, 1906. Her mother signed their marriage license as a witness. Elizabeth stayed in Valentine and took a teaching exam to teach in a rural school. The newly weds returned to the ranch where she continued caring for her younger sister and brothers. She sent them to a nearby rural school - about three miles away. She was a good cook and liked to sew.

Soon Maude kept busy baking bread, making soap, washing on a wash board and caring for their children. William rode his horse to deliver mail to Elsmere. He was helpful with their children and at home. She delivered mail when he was putting up hay. The children graduated from high school, except Paul who after two years quit to help at home and to work out. He figured numbers in his head faster than anyone. His grandson Wayne inherited the math skills without using a pencil or paper as did Ashley.

The Weber family raised a large garden, watered by their windmill. They picked wild berries and greens to supplement the food supply. Maude and Will left the ranch in 1949. She stayed in Arnold until 1961 when she sold out and moved to Lincoln. At 93, Maude had 29 grandchildren, 48 great grand-children and two great great grandchildren. She kept busy making crafts and sewing. Maude lived past 99, born in December 1890 and passed on in March 1990. Services were held in Lincoln and in Arnold with a good turnout at both locations.

Paul and Irene bought the Weber family ranch after his father's death. Roy and Bridget lived in Missouri where they farmed. He died in 2005 at age 97. Lawrence and Ann moved to California where he worked at a steel mill and died in 2001. Chester, a Navy veteran on the Yorktown, was killed in Lincoln when a car ran a stoplight in the spring of 2005. He worked in Wyoming oil fields and on the Burlington Northern Railroad retiring in 1985. Myrle married Ralph Lewis, an Army veteran, of Ainsworth. They moved to Rocca where he auctioneered and ran an 'Opera House' bringing in outstanding entertainers. He played guitar and Marie played an accordion. Myrle died in 2007. Florence Joy sewed curtains in Grand Island and died of lung cancer in 1998. Flora and Leslie Snow retired from the Air Force to Alabama. Flora taught a rural school and was a Registered Nurse. The Weber descendants still gather or call, to share family news and to reminisce.

Grandma kept her mind active and kept in contact by writing to her many family descendants. She knew all her members. She worried about correct spelling and was trying to look words in a dictionary. She said she lost her train of thought in the process. We, her family assured her, she could write words as they sounded and we would figure her meaning. She did and we read her letters fine. She said letter writing was easier without worrying about spelling errors. Grandma was an example of a life well lived.

Weber family in 1922: Grandma Maude, Roy on horse, Lewis, Lawrence, Granddaddy Will holding baby Chester, and Paul on a white horse.

WEBER RECORDS

Christoph Friedrich (Weinartner) Weber was born February 11, 1843 and died May 5, 1929 near Stapleton, Nebraska. He married Jacobina Mack who was born December 19, 1836 in Germany and died December 13, 1917. Both are buried in the McCain Cemetery east of Stapleton where many other family members are also.

He was the son of: Samuel Friederich Weber of Esslingen, Germany and Marie Katharine Bahlinger Schneider (which means tailor). Weber means Weaver, we understood. Jacobina was the daughter of Jakob Mack Schumacher in Untersielmingen, Germany and Christine Alber

Their Kinder-Children: Marie Katharine, born January 9, 1868 and died September 29, 1870, Karoline March14,1869 to August 25,1869; TWINS: Christiane Barbara born December 19, 1869 and died December 9, 1870; Samuel Friederich born December 19, 1869 and died May 1,1954. He married Ada Rogers; TWINS: Marie born October 9, 1870 married to John Rosenthal and died June 23, 1943; Karoline born October 9,1870 married John Schlintz. She died May 3, 1942; Sophie Barbara born March 21, 1872 married Henry Joedeman and died January 29,1940; TWINS: Gustav born April 9, 1873 and died June 29, 1873; Adolf born April 9, 1873 and died November 1, 1873; Andreas Jakob born April 21, 18874 and died May 14, 1874; Jacobina born March 21, 1875 and died March 22, 1875; TWINS: Anonymous totgeb (died at birth); Jakobine born June 5, 1876 and died May 6, 1901; Wilhelm (William) was born May 19, 1877. He married Maude Burris and died October 30, 1953; Christian born June 2, 1878 and died 1955; Jacob born July 18, 1880 married. Anna Greeley. He died May 16, 1945. The family sailed to America in 1879. (We heard the family was ashamed over reports of Hitler and the Holocaust so buried their German coins and things reminiscent of Germany.)

JACOBINA MACK WEBER

Dad's cousin, Caroline Schlintz Clark wrote: "Grandmother was born to a shoemaker, Jacob Mack and Christine Alber in Ober-Esslingen, Germany. To this union 16 children were born, four sets of twins; eight died in infancy. One remained in Germany and one was born in the United States. With six children, the oldest ten these courageous people came to make a new life in 1879. She had much stamina, though she was small of stature, to give birth to so many without doctors. She and Grandfather gave their children a good religious background. Always a prayer of thanksgiving before meals, and an hour of scripture reading, prayers, and song after the evening meal. I recall my mother, aunts and uncles telling what a good mother she was and how they loved her. My mom once told me how she made dye from beet juice, nut shells and roots so they would have colored Easter eggs. I remember what a fine cook she was. She let me unroll the paper thin egg noodles and hang them over a cloth covered chair to dry. The kuchen and brot (cake and bread) were so good. She was neat and her home reeked with cleanliness. She died December 13, 1917 and was interred in in McCain Cemetery near Gandy. May she rest in Peace. Signed Caroline Schlintz Clarke"

CHRISTOPHER F WEBER:

"Grandfather Weber was born to Samuel Friederich Weber, a city employee and Marie Katharine Bahlinger on February 11, 1843 in Ober-Esslingen Germany. On January 22, 1867 he married Jakobina Mack. Due to oppression which affected many lives in Germany, he, his wife and children immigrated to United States and settled in Tower Hill, Illinois. During the Nebraska Homestead Act, he moved his family to Gandy, Nebraska where he lived until his death. Grandfather died May 5, 1929 and is buried Logan County in the McCain Cemetery. The most German Immigrants settled in Illinois and Nebraska ranked second. Credit is due these brave people who had the courage to leave their homeland to travel to a free country. Hardships and language didn't deter them. Thanks, Grandparents for having prudence to move and give us who came after the privilege of living here. Grandfather and his family made an honorable living working the land with no modern equipment. I knew kindness and love which he was endowed with, to know him was to love him. He carried round peppermint candies in his vest pocket which he shared. His visits were looked forward to. Surnames of menfolk were very often known by their occupation, notice Marie K. Bahlinger's father had the name of Schneider attached to his name indicating he was a tailor, which Schneider means. The Weber name means Weaver and apparently someone down the line was a weaver by trade. May God grant him Eternal Rest, Signed, Caroline Schlintz Clarke"

BURRIS

Stacy Burris, was born May 4,1864 and died July 11, 1957 in Wyoming. He lived in Hot Springs County, Thermopolis, Wyoming. Burial was in Washakie County, Worland, Wyoming at Riverview Memorial Gardens. He was a laborer from 1900 to 1938 and in the 1920 Census of Wyoming, Washakie County, Precinct 6 . His obituary is published on July 13, 1957 in Washakie Co, newspaper of Worland, Wyoming. Northern Wyoming Daily News: Thermopolis, reports William Stacy Burris, 93, a resident of Wyoming since 1910, died Thursday at a rest home. Burris was born May 4, 1864, in Indiana and came to Cheyenne in 1910 moving to the Big Horn basin in 1917. He moved to Thermopolis from Winchester about six years ago. He was a retired farmer and inaugurated corn growing on The Down Flats in the early 1920's. Funeral service will be held Monday at 2 P.M. at the Mortimore Chapel; Rev. Glenn Burris will officiate. Burial in Riverview cemetery. He is survived by two sons, Ralph Waldo Burris, Norbuck, Alberta, Canada and Roy Burris, Basin, Wyoming; daughter, Maude Weber, Arnold, Nebraska,16 grandchildren, 52 great grandchildren and one great great grandchild. One daughter Florence and his wife Elizabeth preceded him in death. Marriage: Elizabeth Kathryn Lewellen born September 22,1868, died June 1953 and is buried in the cemetery south of Arnold, Nebraska.

Children:

1. Maude Louellen Burris born December 15, 1890 in Guthrie County, Bagley, Iowa

2. Florence Burris born January 18, 1893 in Dallas County, Redfield, Iowa

3. Ralph Waldo Burris born September 17, 1895 in Dallas County, Linden, Iowa

4. Roy Stanton Burris born April 8, 1899 in Dallas County, Redfield, Iowa

GRANDMA PAINE

Grandma was a lady. She dressed in clean pressed dresses, white gloves and a hat, when she was in public. She acted like a lady and never talked rough. She was wise and expected us, her nine grandchildren to act proper. She often talked about her mother and her large family of brothers and sisters. Grandma lived by example.

My Grandma did not have an easy life. She was born in England and came to America with seven brothers and sisters when small. Her health was so poor that there was talk of tossing her body into the ocean on the three month trip. She was the middle of 13 and was a happy jolly person. She often laughed and giggled causing us to laugh with her.

My grandma began working as a midwife, to help women giving birth, when she was young. She told me about going in a horse pulled buggy to attend births no matter the weather or time, day or night. She often stayed all night waiting, giving reassurance to the mother-to-be. She told me about some who did not survive. She shared compassion with families of deformed infants destined to die.

At 26, Grandma married Grandpa. She told me, "Don't marry the first man who asks you, I didn't!" (I didn't either.) A year later she delivered their first baby, my mother, in their little sod home. She told me she had a long painful three days of very hard labor.

Years sped by and the family moved about a hundred miles north to live in a sod house near Stapleton. After three years they moved again to the remote Nebraska Sandhills. They traveled in a horse-drawn wagon loaded. A milk cow and a horse followed. My mother said at six, she rode on the sled and held her cat on the four day trip. She remembered stopping at a bachelor's home where Grandma baked biscuits in his chimney oven. He was happy for company and a good cook.

Grandma maintained her dignity in another sod home keeping it clean and comfortable with an organ, crocheted and embroidered pillows and a striking clock. Water was pumped outside into a well house and carried in to heat on a wood-burning range.

Our grandparents operated the Elizabeth Post Office in their home for years. She told me it was not an easy job. Ranchers came tromping through for their mail, wearing their muddy, corral dirtied overshoes, dirtying her clean mopped floor. Pay for operating the Post Office service was free mailing privileges for packages. Nothing more.

I remember walking in the pastures with Grandma, while quite small. We picked up dry cow chips for her range stove for cooking. We hauled them in a small hand pulled wagon, to build a good fire. Wood was not plentiful in the hills.

Grandma milked cows, drove horses pulling haying machinery and helped however she could on the ranch. When I visited as a child, I waited outside the double hinged barn door while she milked their cows. A gentle horse reached his head over the door and snorted on my head. He scarred the wits out of me! I yelled. Grandma checked, then continued milking while laughing 'til tears rolled down her cheeks.

The Paine's second child, daughter Mildred was born, January 10, 1920, while Grandma was alone in their sod home. My mother - 11, was told to knead the bread dough and make loaves, 'to keep her in the kitchen.' Grandma said she delivered her baby herself quickly on the sofa. She was amazed at the speedy delivery this time. Grandpa was outside doing chores.

Communication was primarily the every other day mail carrier, when they could come. They brought cards and letters from friends and relatives. She sorted mail into cubicles in the roll top desk for the neighbors. When tragedy struck, word was spread by a horse back rider.

Grandma chose not to live alone on the ranch after Grandpa died of pneumonia. She sold their big herd of horses, machinery and all she didn't think she'd need, which was everything- dishes, tools, animals and vehicles. She moved in with us 'to help.' I still recall Ted and I having fun pulling that single horse buggy around the yard during the auction. Grandma said she rode in that buggy many times to deliver babies. Wouldn't we enjoy having that buggy now?

Home remedies were a specialty of Grandma's. She looked after everyone, insisting my brothers, sister and I put Vicks on our necks at night and wrap them with long stockings, if our throats were sore. She was always concerned about her high blood pressure. She and Grandpa raised a big garden. I helped pick potato bugs off by carrying a little can of kerosene to put the bugs in. They brought asparagus and other produce to share in season when they drove over the trail roads to visit. Grandma looked for edible weeds, as lambs quarters, to cook in the early spring.

Grandma wrote long interesting letters to her family. She and her sisters exchanged flower blossoms, sitting on them to press. She visited and helped where she felt she could. In later years Grandma couldn't see, her eyes were fogged with cataracts. She was 90 and nearly blind so she hired a lady to make a quilt for her youngest great granddaughter, Kristi Irene.

My grandma was a busy country lady; her hands were never idle. She made beautiful hand stitched 'flower garden' quilts for each of her four granddaughters. She worked new material into flower designs with carefully planned colors for each. She learned to use an electric sewing machine though she said she didn't like it. "It goes too fast 'brrr' this way and 'brrr' that way," she laughed, her brown eyes twinkling. She was serious but kept sewing until she mastered that machine. She machine sewed quilts for her grandsons.

Grandma spent her final ten years in the Valentine nursing home because she fell and broke her hip and could no longer navigate. The week before she fell, she was out riding with my young sons on the sand buggy my dad built. She held on laughing and enjoying her great grandsons Jerry and Wayne driving. She had a great time joking as she rode. In the nursing home, Grandma wrote letters to her children and grandchildren. She often wrote, "It's too dark to see in here." She didn't know her cataracts darkened her world. Grandma never used rough language or showed impropriety even when wheel chair bound. I took her picture and she managed to rise from the wheel chair to stand in the picture.

My Grandma reminded me often of her mother's words, "Remember if you ever get to Manchester, England, tell them you are a descendant of Tindale and you will be well treated." (William Tindale was burned at stake for translating the Bible into English so the common people could read it. His dying words were a prayer, "Lord open the King of England's eyes." The King James version of the Bible, printed in 1611, was the answer to Tindale's prayer.) Grandma said her mother told her she had ancestors who came to England with William the Conquerer, in 1066.

Grandma was a lady and much more. She was respected and admired for her lively sense of humor, intelligence, caring ways, complete composure, beautiful white hair and sterling character. She continued helping others as long as she was able. She lived six weeks short of 96. She visited all her grandchildren and their families who loved and respected her. She outlived all but two of her 12 siblings and they traveled great distances to honor and remember her despite the extreme cold January weather, for final services in Valentine. She and Grandpa are buried in Mount Hope Cemetery in Wood Lake. We smile through tears at their legend of love which lingers.

AUNT LETTIE'S CUP

An old ceramic cup, minus a handle, was a family keepsake for near one hundred fifty years. It was that and much more. The white cup's history reaches back to the Civil War when each soldier and nurse was allotted a multi-use white mug. Nurses were given the mug with their provisions the same as the men.

This aged inanimate mug in my cupboard was given to a young nurse named Melissa Covell, known as Lettie, when she left home, without telling her family, to help in the Civil War effort. She wrote her mother upon arriving: "I hope you will understand, Mother, that I had to leave and to do what I could to help our injured soldiers." The cup was her tool to feed soldiers, give them a drink of cool water and for a shaving mug.

Lettie remained in the service for several years traveling where needed. When she returned to California, she left the cup with her sister Minerva in Nebraska. It remained buried in an old trunk over a hundred years. When her sister's possessions were sorted the cup was given to other descendants.

Another reason Lettie joined the service was to locate her brother Marcellus J. Covell, who had not been heard from for too long. He was later declared killed in action. His Sergent wrote her parents and sister Minerva Paine, in answer to letters of inquiry. The letter said he was killed instantly by a bullet and given a decent burial nearby.

Relatives have Marcellus' old diaries where he wrote of hardships in the service. His first assignment was to recruit volunteer soldiers. He wrote about sleeping in barns and walking through the countryside to find recruits to serve the country. He wrote of his successes and discouragements as he trained and served valiantly.

It was a long time before troops were allotted horses and ammunition. Marcellus wrote they had to wash their white gloves for a parade in Chicago. He told of riding over rough terrain through the south, picking fruit for sustenament. He found it tough waiting for letters from home. He kept an account of all his expenses down to a few cents spent for postage.

A Sergent, who wrote to M.J. Covell's parents said, "Sgt. Covell's possessions were lost when he was hospitalized." Then he was in a skirmish and shot. Lettie continued to be an adventurous lady. One letter reported she rode a roller coaster in California. The old ceramic mug was in my cupboard for nearly 50 years then it was stolen. Sharing stories should make us aware of sacrifices made to make this country great. We pray for strength and intelligence to keep our soldiers safe and our country prosperous.

GREAT GRANDMA PAINE
By Elsie M. Paine

Grandma (Minerva) Paine was the youngest in the family of seven children of Thomas and Elizabeth Brown Covell. Her parents were pioneers, living near Chicago when it was still Fort Dearborn. Her father died of lung fever caused by a tree falling on him while he was helping fight a forest fire, while she was a very small girl.

The family continued living on the family farm for some years. When Grandma was 12, she and her mother moved to live with her oldest sister, Mary Eastman, and husband, Ruben, in Iowa where she later met her future husband, Cassius Paine. She returned to Illinois to attend school and on November 30, 1865, she and Cassius were married. After two years they returned to Auburn, Fayette County, Iowa, where they lived for ten years. Then they moved to Harlan County in Nebraska. They and all their possessions came by rail to Republican City, Nebraska, the end of the rails. They came the rest of the way by wagon.

Minerva was rather a small person with blue eyes and dark hair. A schoolmate thought Minerva too long a name for such a small girl and nicknamed her Nellie, from her second name, Cornelia. She was known as Nellie from then on by family and friends. She was very hospitable. I don't think any one ever visited them, regardless of the time of day, that she didn't immediately start preparing a meal.

She loved to tell stories of her parent's early days as she heard them from her mother. A favorite was of a threatened Indian attack. Her father was away and her mother alone, with her two oldest children, who were very young. Chief Shabonna came to warn them to go to the fort. He took little Mary on his horse in front of him, Elizabeth, holding the baby, mounted behind him and he took them to Fort Dearborn.

The settlers rushed to the fort for safety so hurriedly that they ran low on food. Elizabeth volunteered to go out to the scattered cabins and collect supplies, with help of a young boy, she did. The women in the fort felt that she would be killed and wept when she left assuring her they would care for her children. She returned with a wagon load of supplies.

Grandma remembered how the Indians, on their way to collect Government pensions in later years, always stopped at their home. Her mother was very strict about her children's behavior toward them, treating them with kindness and courtesy at all times. Indians picked apples in the Covell orchard and swam nude in the creek—which she especially disliked.

(Minerva Cornelia Covell, born at Proviso, Cook County, Illinois on February 28, 1843, married Cassius Marcellus Clay Paine at Lyonsville, Illinois. They were parents of Mertie Elizabeth 1867—1943, Charlie Bruce 1870—1917, Edith Minerva 1906—1910, Mary Maud 1875—1957 and Claude Seth, April 6,1881 to April 4,1943. The family brought with them a walnut chest of drawers, her father had made, in a covered wagon from Illinois to Iowa and finally on to Nebraska. Aunt Mildred got the chest, as my mother said, It is family tradition the youngest granddaughter should inherit the chest. Mildred had the chest refinished. Cousin Jeanie will be the next in line to inherit the lovely antique solid walnut chest of drawers.)

OBITUARY

Mary Hoyt, daughter of Heman and Susan Hoyt, was born in St. Albams, Vermont on August 2, 1817. Removed with her parents west in 1836. She married Dr. F.S. Payne on September 19,1841. Five children were born to them George, Cassius, Albert, Fulwer and Lois. George gave his life for his country, Albert is supposed dead, Cassius and Fulwer reside in Nebraska and Lois Houston is in Rockford, Illinois at whose home the mother passed away. She was the eldest of nine children. Three brothers, Timothy, Oliver and Heman Hoyt and two sisters, Cynthia Campbell and Louise Humphrey survive her. She had long wished to depart to her better home where she felt sure she would meet all her loved ones gone. She believed in the salvation of all mankind as God's children. Selfishness and unkindness were strangers to her nature. Always thinking of others—seldom of self. Was respected by all who knew her. She passed to that home not made with hands, eternal in the heavens on the 15th of October 1902, after a long and useful life, aged 85 years, two months and three days. She was borne to her final resting place beside her loved parents with tenderest care by her nephews, Nelson, Timothy, Casper and Heman Hoyt and Romeo and Jerrie Campbell. Kind friends showed by their presence their respect for one of the pioneers of Illinois. Rev. Chas. Kramer of Galesburg, Illinois. officiated. Singing was by Mrs. Clarence Atwood and Miss Florence Walker of Durand. J.M. Gerry, Undertaker.

"I have passed from the shadow of sadness.

Into the sunshine of gladness,

Into the light of the blest,

Into a joy land above us

Where there's a Father to love us—

Into our "Home-Sweet Home."

Name   Elijah Paine

Birth   January 21 1757, Pomfret, Connecticut

Death   April 21, 1842

Occupation Vermont Supreme Court Judge, U.S. Senator, U.S. District Judge

Education   Harvard College 1781 University of Vermont, 1825

Father   Seth Paine 1719-1792

Mother   Mabel Tyler 1724-1792

Spouse   Sarah Porter

Death   May 31, 1851

Marriage   June 7, 1790

Children   Sarah 1792-1795

            Martyn 1794-1877

            Elijah 1796-1853

            Charles 1799-1854

            Caroline 1801-

            Sophia 1803-

            George 1807-1836

Elijah Paine, born January 21, 1757 Graduated from Harvard College in 1781 He was admitted to the bar to practice law in Windsor, Vermont and served in the Revolutionary War. In 1785, he was one of the first settlers in Montpelier, Vermont and cleared the first land in Northfield. He was engaged as an agriculturist and established a cloth factory merchant at Windsor. In 1787 he moved to Williamstown, where he resided through a long eventful life, highly respected for his various talents. In 1790 he was appointed one of the committee to settle the boundary line between the states of Vermont and New York. He was a senator in congress in 1795 when they met in Philadelphia and re-elected in 1801. He was appointed by President John Adams to the office of Judge of the District Court of Vermont, where he stayed until just before his death. On June 7, 1790 he married Sarah Porter of Williamstown who died May 31, 1851, having had eight children. Elijah died April 21, 1842 leaving four sons and two daughters: Martyn, Elijah, Charles, George, Caroline and Sophia. Interment: West Hill Cemetery Williamstown.

An anecdote of him from D. P. Thompson's History of Montpelier, Vermont, as related by Josiah Benjamin, Esq., on page 53: "In the winter of 1786 Elijah Paine and a distant neighbor started with each a load of grain for Boston. The snow was nearly five feet deep, and it was almost impossible to turn out. In going through Brookfield, in one of the worst places, we met a team loaded with salt; finding there was no possibility of getting by each other, except by unloading all our sleighs, and then turning them side ways in the snow-walled path, and so running them by empty, we all fell to, unloaded the three sleighs, and run the man's sleigh past ours. As it happened we loaded up his sleigh first and got him ready to start.

"Judge Paine and myself then turned back for the purpose of loading up our teams, expecting of course that the stranger would assist us. But the next instant we heard the loud crack of his whip, and saw the fellow mounted on his sleigh, lashing his horses to escape and leave us to load up our own sleighs. Judge Paine looked after the pitiful fugitive for but an instant with eyes that fairly flashed fire. Suddenly dashing off his hat and great coat, he gave chase on foot, running as I thought I never saw any one run before, until he overtook the team. When he leaped like a tiger upon the load of salt, seized the shrinking puppy by the collar, and made a flying leap with him sideways into the snow. He then drew his prisoner into the road, and led him back to our loads; when, giving him a mighty significant push towards our bags of wheat still lying untouched in the snow, he coolly, and with that sort of curt, dignified politeness, which even in moments of anger rarely forsook him, observed, 'There friend, if you will take hold of these bags, and load up both of our sleighs, we will be much obliged to you, very much obliged to you sir.' The fellow sheepishly did so to the last bag, the judge not permitting me to lend the least assistance. We then drove on, leaving him to the comfortable reflection which the incident might suggest to him."

An anecdote concerning Judge Paine's wife, Sarah, a lady of literary as well as domestic accomplishments. "In the year 1785 or 86, Prince Edward, son of the bigoted and muddy-brained King George II and a true chip of the old block, traveled from Montreal to Boston, with a guard of 15 or 20 armed attendants to protect him, and several tasters to taste and eat a portion of food before he would venture to touch it. "He stopped at Judge Paine's house at Williamstown, Vermont, for his dinner, and was disposed to be chatty and jocose. Among his witty efforts, he said to Mrs. Paine, 'I suppose madam that you have never read any thing but your Bible and Psalm book?' 'Oh yes, we do, sir,' promptly replied Mrs. Paine, 'We are all quiet familiar with the writings of one Peter Pindar.' Those who have read the scorching satires of Pindar on the character and capacities of the then royal family will readily appreciate the keenness of Madam Paine's retort." Reference: Paine Family Record - A Quarterly Magazine 1880-1883 by Henry D. Paine - reprint through The New England Historical Genealogical Society, Elijah graduated from Harvard in 1781, was Judge of the Supreme Court of Vermont, 1791 to 1794, U.S. Senator, 1794 to 1801, and U.S. District Judge, 1801 to 1842. He was a Fellow of the American Academy, and LL.D. (Harvard, 1812, University. of Vermont, 1825). Res. Williamstown, Vermont. Reference: History of Woodstock, Connecticut (Genealogies of Woodstock Families) by Clarence W. Bowen 1943 Vol 8[14]

GRANDMA'S 1914 LETTER

I read letters written by my Grandma Paine to his parents, Cassius and Minerva, in Oxford, Nebraska. The Paine's were close, yet they did things that surprised me. Minerva, Cassius and son Charlie attended the Chicago World's Fair in 1893, each traveling separately. Travel was easy on trains though it would be a long trip. They wrote home telling their daughters/sisters where they were and who they were visiting. The sisters kept their letters.

Grandpa rode a bicycle, while quite young, to Lexington, Nebraska. Roads would have been dry, dusty and rough. I learned this from a journal written by his sister, Maud.

Claude and Etta and Irene, moved from Oxford by team pulling a hay sled loaded with their possessions, a cow and horse following, to a ranch just west of Stapleton with Claude's Uncle Fulwar Paine. Fulwar and Aunt Ellen had William, George, and Lois. The mother taught them in a rural Logan County school. Claude took his horse and rifle riding in the Sandhills looking for a ranch to buy. They lived in a sod house near Stapleton for three years.

In 1916 the Paine family moved to Cherry County with some Angus cattle, a horse and a few chickens. My mother said she rode on the sled and held her cat while the dog and a milk cow followed. They stopped at night at places along the way. Mom remembered playing with little children and their new baby chickens on one stop. Grandma moved from one sod house to another. I stayed all night with my grandparents in their sod house which leaked when it rained. Grandma set out pans to catch rain drops. Grandpa worked putting up hay with horses and raising his Angus cattle—before black cattle were accepted in the region.

My parents met when they began school together in District 102. She kept valentines Dad and his brothers had made for her written on tablet paper with a pencil.

April 23, 1914

Stapleton

Dear Mother and All,

I feel as if I ought to write you a few lines to let you know that we are getting along fine and are all well. Claude got yours and Mertie's letters and enjoyed reading every word. I don't know when he will be ready to answer. We were glad to hear that Maud is feeling better. She must have had a long siege.

Irene was real excited when she heard about your chickens. Twelve of our Plymouth Rock eggs hatched over a week ago. The hogs got one but we have eleven fine little chicks left. And five hens setting, our hens are in no hurry to set.

We have had some terrible windy days the past two weeks but yesterday, Wednesday, was the worst of all. It blew up a shower in the evening and has been coming in showers all day. The sand drifted two feet high in front of the south door and the porch is loaded with sand. So if you should come be sure to come to the east door. I have a hen setting on the front porch and also keep the chickens there. It is screened in so they can't blow away.

We have three boxes of tomatoes plants in the south window up and doing fine. Also some California flower seeds. They came up but don't look very strong. The hills are beginning to look quite green and rye and alfalfa are showing up fine. But most of the rye was killed this winter. Claude and his hired man are sorting over potatoes this after noon We bought what Uncle had to spare and hope we can get some planted soon. Mr. Gibbs and Bakewells were planting spuds yesterday.

We fixed up the cream separator this morning and are going to milk a few cows as soon as their calves can get on grass. Have only milked one of Roanies heifers this winter. We have six all black baby calves. Claude bought eight calves at the sale so we have nearly as many as Uncle had when he sold out. Little White Face has stood the winter the best of any of them. And she is as pretty and gentle.

One of Claude's young sows has been awfully sick. They started to haul her off, thinking she was dead. But as she showed signs of life, they thought they would leave her another day. She has been getting better ever since and is walking among this alfalfa looking for something to eat. She has sores on her back. The others are doing fine. They run all over the place. Claude hasn't fed them any corn yet.

The men have been working over the Claim every day the last two weeks. They built a two wire fence all around the place and made the wind mill tower and put it up. He has a neat little sod house and a good frame barn and well. You know he has only rented this place for one year. I don't know what he intends to do about the claim. The Miss Bright land was sold last month and people are breaking there now. They come here every day for water and to borrow something and want fifteen cents worth of eggs when they are 14 a dozen. They have eight children and most of them red headed. Mr. Brincomb is red headed too… I am going to keep still about my nationality.

Mrs. Advent Preacher Johnson was here the other day. Her son had just come home from Lincoln. Are they any relation of yours?

I have been pretty busy cleaning up the house since Aunt Ellen left. I think a sod house is so hard to keep clean. It seems nice to have plenty of room even if we haven't much to put in the house. We got a 10 ½ by 12 foot ingrain rug and a sink at Sears R and Co. Both are nice. I want to sew our rags up for a rag carpet rug for the kitchen as soon as I get time. I can't scrub such a big floor. We got a nice big letter from Fannie, (a sister) the same time we got yours and five others. I was so glad but time is going so fast and none of them answered yet. Route three has news for us this week. Claude doesn't expect to get paid for the wind mill.

Irene is taking a nap. She says when she gets to be a big girl she will take her own naps. She hates to take them now. Pauline (an aged tin headed doll that belonged to her cousin Edith) and her are as chummie as ever but she likes to be out of doors with Uncle.

Mertie asked what the name of Mr Bronson's Poem was. It think it was called, The Situation of Today. I cut a strand of baby's hair for her a long time ago but forgot to sent it before.

P.S. heard from Mrs. F.S. yesterday. He says she expects to start for West Virginia today to visit the Dye's. William graduates in three weeks so she will be back in time for that. They are talking of selling the auto and going west on the train now. So I don't know what they will do. Lois wants to visit at Omaha. Her beau is there, and SD. Before she goes west. I expect Uncle Fulwar will be with us about a month yet. He says he is going to put in his time fixing up things, Well, I guess I must close and get supper ready. I hope this finds you all well and that you will write soon or come see us. With Love from All, Etta Paine

P.S. We had two prairie roosters for dinner. (The letter was postmarked April 28, 1914 Stapleton, Nebraska. My mom was five. Outside the envelope, addressed to Mrs. C.M. Paine Oxford, Nebraska, it says: "Answered May 11 to 14, 1914. I wrote 23 pages and Mother five," in Aunt Maud's distinctive handwriting.)

THOMAS REED COVELL

Copied from
"Genealogy and History of Cook County, Illinois"

Thomas R. Covell bore a character so marked in its impress upon the times in which he lived that few parallels are afforded by contemporary history. While his life was filled with many dangers and hardships of a realistic kind, there centered about him, in his varied career, much that was romantic, tingeing his life with a glow which brings out in bold relief the indomitable characteristics of an heroic soul, one endowed by nature with all the requisites of mind and purpose to make a successful pioneer.

To become a way-blazer into the heart of a wilderness, where dangers lurk and want stalks unchecked and unopposed, required courage greater than usually falls to the lot of men. The mental, moral and physical makeup of Thomas Reed Covell constituted him to become more than a trail-blazer. While he was courageous enough to lead, he had, as well, the fixedness of purpose to carve out a home in the unsubdued wilds of a remote frontier.

He was a New Englander by birth, born in the year 1800, in West Stockbridge, Massachusetts. His father was a native of Paris, France and came to America with General La Fayette to take part on the side of the struggling colonists against the tyranny of England. Under his renowned leader he bore the part of a gallant soldier, and on an expedition against the Indian allies of the British was taken prisoner by the savage foe. He was tried according to the methods of his captors and given fourteen days to live. Fourteen marks were placed on his forehead and at each revolution of the sun a mark was removed; but before the last mark was reached he was taken in charge by the British army and imprisoned at Quebec, where he remained eighteen months in confinement. After the declaration of peace Henry Covell, born in 1747, married, Polly Reed, a native of New York, of English descent, and subsequently settled in Massachusetts, where they made a permanent home.

Thomas R. Covell was reared on a farm in the state of his nativity. He developed early in life a disposition for adventure and when he was nineteen years old he went out from the parental home to seek his fortune in the West. New Orleans was his objective point, which he made his appearance in 1819. Indians roamed the country at will; but, nothing daunted, he plunged still deeper into the wilds, locating temporarily at St. Louis. Thence he went to Peoria, Illinois and returned to Missouri where he followed hunting and trapping on the "American Bottoms." Subsequently he engaged in the fur business, buying and trafficking with the Indians, disposing of his purchases in New Orleans. In this business he was engaged about nineteen years, having lived during that time in St. Louis, Peoria, Ottawa and Plainfield.

In 1828, while living in Peoria, he married Elizabeth, daughter of James Brown. Mr. Brown was also a pioneer and a native of Philadelphia, Pennsylvania.

In 1832, during the Black Hawk war, Mr. Covell was living with his family at Plainfield, Illinois. The white people were in imminent danger, as roving warlike bands of Indians were devastating the settlements in all directions. Mr. Covell had the confidence of the red men and was the cherished friend of the renowned chief, Shabonna, of the Pottawatomie and other distinguished Indians. During these exciting days some mounted Indians appeared at his door and informed Mr. Covell that an attack was about to be made upon the settlement. They asked for fresh horses that they might give warning to other settlers, as well as bring friendly Indians to the rescue. Mr. Covell's horse was exhausted by recent reconnaissance of the situation, but he went at once to a neighbor, from whom horses were obtained, and their dusky friends went on their errand of mercy. These friendly savages told Mr. Covell to take his departure as soon as the squaws began taking down the wigwams. They said, "White man's throat be cut by bad Indians." Needless to say, Mr. Covell acted on this advice and quickly departed with his family for the protecting walls of Fort Dearborn, where they remained from June until October, 1832.

The commander of the fort recognized in Mr. Covell a leader and commissioned him captain in the militia service. His Indian friends remained true to him during the time he was in the fort and furnished him valuable information as to the movements of the enemy, informing him at one time of a carefully planned attack upon the fort to be made at three o'clock in the morning. This attack was not made, however, for the reason the attacking party discovered that complete preparations had been made for repelling the onslaught. They retired with the cry, "Cho-ka-kote." The name of the city is a corrupted form of the word, "Cho-ka-koke, not worth taking. "The Chicago River was known to the Indians by the name of "Scakote," so called because of the innumerable skunks that infested the river.

After the treaty of peace had been signed, Mr. Covell returned to his home on Covell Creek near Plainfield. The following year, in October 1833, he settled on section 28, Proviso Township, Cook County, where he developed a farm, residing thereon the rest of his natural life, and becoming identified with many of the offices of the township. He was a man of indomitable courage and great steadfastness of purpose.

Covell feared no foe and never turned his back to a friend, white or red. These traits endeared him to his dusky neighbors. He was the first and only man of that day to successfully trade with the Sioux. Upon his first visit to this tribe, in company with four others in his employ, he carried a pack, which a thieving Indian undertook to steal, beside offering him other indignities. He defended his property in such a vigorous way that the Indians applauded him vociferously and ever afterward they were his friends.

Mr. Covell was about 5 feet 10 inches in height, inclined to spareness and of perfect physical development. His hair was black and curling, his eyes blue and piercing, of medium complexion, and in health weighted about 150 pounds. He was of a nervous temperament, capable of great endurance, never giving way to fatigue. His estimable wife partook largely of her husband's nature, and entered fully with him into his undertakings and heroically bore her part in all that for so many years surrounded their home. To them were born eight children, namely: Manda, who died in infancy; Mary J—Mrs. Reuben Eastman, Marisa C., of La Grange, Illinois; Maria—Mrs. Philander Ingersoll, of Waverly, Iowa; Melissa, a Civil War nurse, married James Buckley of Chicago; Marcellus J., who served as a member of Company F. Ninth Illinois Cavalry, with the rank of Regimental Surgeon and was killed in the battle of Chambersville, Tennessee in 1864; and Minerva—Mrs. Cassius Paine of Nebraska. Thomas Reed Covell died October 1846 at age 46. Elizabeth Brown Reed, his wife, departed this life in Iowa in

1867 at 66 years. His remains lie interred in Oak Hill Cemetery, on land he donated.

THOMAS REED COVELL
Condensed from family DAR record

Thomas Reed Covell sold furs and traded with the Indians. He was the first and only man of that day who traded successfully with the Indians. While in Ottawa, he built a small log cabin and remained there long enough to assist in building a saw and grist mill for James Walker, the saw mill still stands in 2010. The old buildings of Chicago were constructed of black walnut timbers which was the principal lumber sawed at the Ottawa Mill and at Walker's Mill for a very long time. Chicago received building materials from there.

Early farmers depended on sawmills to build barns, large frame homes and eventually, community centers. The building of James Walker's Mill marked the beginning of the village of Plainfield. Thomas R. Covell and his family lived in Plainfield during the 1832 Black Hawk War. Roving Indians were attacking and devastating settlements in all directions and pioneers were in imminent danger. Thomas R. Covell won the confidence of Native Americans and was a cherished friend of Shabonna, renowned Pottawatomie Chief.

During the Black Hawk War these friendly Indians told Thomas Covell to leave with his family as soon as the squaws take down their wigwams. They said, "White man's throat be cut by bad Indians!" Thomas Covell acted on their advice and fled immediately with his family to Fort Dearborn in Chicago.

Accommodations were extremely crowded in Chicago as fugitives came from outlying settlements. In their hasty flight, most settlers didn't have time to bring supplies and little was to be found in Chicago. It seemed there were two choices, be scalped, or starve.

A muster roll for the Black Hawk War included Thomas Reed Covell as private. He later became Captain of the Volunteers. The volunteers were mustered out of service on August 12, 1832, each drawing their land warrants, but Thomas Reed Covell remained at the fort until October 1832. His Indian friends remained true while he was at the fort and furnished him with valuable information about movement of the enemy.

PAINES

By Howard C. Paine

Cassius (Cash) Marcellus Clay Paine and Minerva Cornelia (Nellie) Paine are my grandparents. Grandfather Paine came from a pioneer family centered in New York. Seth appears in Dutches County, said by Eliza Paine Shafer to be a cousin of Thomas Paine. His son Abijah and other sons were supervisors of Davenport Township.

His second child, Dr. Fulwar Skepwith Paine, of whom we descended, was born at Delhi, Delaware County. New York on August 12, 1805. He died in East Saginaw, Michigan, November 16, 1865. He went to Illinois as a young man and married Mary Orton Hoit on September 25, 1845. Their daughter Ann Eliza was Imogene Shafer's mother. Gene lived in Beatrice, Nebraska for many years. Fulwar and Mary Paine later separated. Mertie Paine said he was a rather cold stern man. Fulwar and Mary's second son was Cassius, my grandfather was born August 16, 1845 near Durand, Winnebago County, Illinois. Cassius married Minerva Cornelia Covell of Chicago, which was called Fort Dearborn. Her father Thomas R. Covell, was a pioneer settler and fur trader with the Indians in the area and along the Mississippi.

When we visited Grandma Paine, as youngsters, she told us about early days when at least two occasions her mother and her young family had to flee to the fort because of Indian uprisings. Her mother was a rather strong woman and earned a reputation for bravery in her own right. I don't know where Thomas Reed was but I believe with the militia. She was kindly and thoughtful, worshiped by her husband and family. When I knew her, she was somewhat dominated by her daughter Mertie, the schoolteacher and brighter daughter. Grandma was interested in people and loved to have relatives visit. She thought lemon juice would cure any ailment. She was only three when her father died. There was some feeling that the eventual disposition of the La Grange estate, which largely went to the boys, was not fair to her or her sisters. As young grandchildren, my two sisters, (Elsie and Nell) and I were something special and always the center of attention when we visited.

Memories of my father are few and far between. My mother, Frances Vasey, was the teacher at Pleasant Valley School, in Harlan County, and stayed with the Paine family during her teaching career. Hence she came to know the Paines very well and when my father asked to marry her, there was no hesitation in saying, "Yes." She was 23 and he was 31 when they were wed in Alma, Nebraska. My father asked my Grandfather Vasey if he could marry his daughter and was reported to have replied, "She is the best I have, but take her and be good to her." They established their home on the hills above Grandfather Paine's farm where my sisters and I were born. My father grew up in open Nebraska country and loved to hunt and fish. He was a friendly open person with a sense of humor, actually jolly, and devoted to his wife and family. Perhaps he was somewhat of a self satisfied hard worker, the family was reasonably prosperous on their little farm and were planning to buy an automobile, 1917, when his untimely death occurred. He was almost 47 years. This is the Paine heritage—English and French and very patriotic Americans. They were proud of their heritage.

GEORGE VASEY

Compendium of History, Reminiscence and Biography of Western Nebraska, 1909

One of the most enthusiastic, intelligent and successful farmers in Harlan County is the gentleman above named, and by his thrift and industry has accumulated a valuable estate, consisting of two hundred and forty acres, on which he has a handsome house fitted up with every modern convince, including heat, bath with hot and cold water connections, etc. His farm is located in Eldorado township, and the soil is all good river bottom and second bottom land, on which he is able to raise banner crops of all kinds. He is treasurer of the Harlan County Agricultural Association, with the fair grounds at Alma, and one of the up-to-date, progressive men of his county.

Mr. Vasey is a native of Yorkshire, England and was raised on his father's farm there, the latter coming to America with his family many years ago, and settling in Nebraska in 1885, where he died in 1926, at age of seventy. George Vasey farmed in Christian County, Illinois, for several years before locating here, and from there moved to Gage County, this state, for six years. His experience with the methods and soils of those places have been of great value to him in his agriculture pursuits here, and he considers, taking every thing into account, that the Republican Valley is far ahead of any place he has ever seen. Since coming here he has made a special study of corn culture, and firmly believes in "thoroughbred corn," that each farmer should select the best possible seed and plant a patch by itself for seed, and in this patch he should pull out all the non-bearing stalks, as otherwise these will fertilize the others and much of the seed will thus be non-productive. It is his nature to study thoroughly whatever subject he has on hand, and in this way he reaches the best possible results in each part of his work.

Mr. Vasey first located in Harlan County in 1893, paying two thousand five hundred and fifteen dollars for his land, and at the present time it is worth more than fifteen thousand dollars, which is good evidence of the advance which has taken place throughout this part of the state in the past few years, due entirely to the efforts of such farmers and business men as our subject. He runs fifty to one hundred high grade cattle on his farm, and about one hundred to two hundred hogs. He crosses Shorthorn cattle with the Red Polled, the former being his favorite for milk and beef. He feeds his calves flax meal, preparing them for market the first season, and sells them at an average price of fifty dollars per head, thus making a good profit. Whereas he figures that keeping them for two or three years and then selling at seventy five dollars per head is not making as much money. There are fine springs on his place for his stock, and he also has a splendid irrigation ditch in operation. To keep his farm free from grasshoppers he always keeps a number of guinea fowls, and finds this a very effective method of keeping pests down.

Mr. Vasey was married in 1868 to Miss Margaret Tindale. To them have been born thirteen children. In 1895, Mr. Vasey was elected justice of the peace and at present is serving as chairman of the Eldorado township board, having been a member of that board for some years. He is also on the school board, and one of the active members of that body.

George and Margaret Vasey with ten of their children at Alma, Nebraska in 1909, before their return trip to England.

TINDALE-VASEY

Margaret sat beside her grandmother watching carefully as she skillfully worked her needle in and out. Margaret tried hard to make stitches as neat like her grandmother's. She used her thimble as she was taught. But Margaret lacked practice.

It was cool and the logs in the big fireplace crackled cheerfully as lamps cast a flickering eerie glow around the large nearly bare castle room. Margaret and Grandmother Tindale sat on padded benches built in castle walls near the fire for warmth and comfort. Grandfather William Tindale sat nearby resting, after a day's work caring for the castle grounds.

Margaret, an attractive girl with curly brown hair and brown eyes with golden flecks of light in them, was born in Manchester, England. She was raised by grandparents as her mother passed away before she could remember. Her father, a joiner by trade, died at age 41, leaving Margaret, a four years old, to live with her grandparents in the old castle in Brompton. Grandmother taught Margaret to cook, knit, crochet and sew. They spent evenings sewing and visiting by lamp light. A close bond continued as Grandmother repeated stories of family and events of long ago and the day's happenings. Margaret's brother Jon disappeared and was thought murdered on the Kings' Highway—the Thames River. Her brother Wiley and sister Agnes were grown and some cousins lived in Riffin—one was a grocer.

Grandmother said her ancestors came from Normandy with William the Conqueror, the first Norman king of England who built Windsor Castle in 1066. Margaret heard of William Tindale who translated the King James version of the Bible. "He was a distant relative and a fine looking man with dark wavy hair, educated in higher places of England and Germany." He attended Oxford University and was associated with Martin Luther. He was a Christian whose desire was to translate the Bible into the language common people could read. William Tindale (Tyndale) was burned at stake for his faith in 1536.

Margaret played near castle walls, where she watched older children run, climb and jump. An older child landed on her, a jolt was so severe Margaret remembered it years later. When chores were completed, Margaret rode with her Grandfather as he took his horse drawn buggy on errands about town. Margaret noticed how the horse made its way without guiding reins. She innocently asked, "How is it that the horse knows where to go?" Grandfather Tindale laughed, confiding, "I whisper directions in his ear."

At 14, Margaret was confirmed in Saint Mary's Episcopal Church in Brompton. She continued to dedicate her life to faith. Her faith was a strong thread of stability through the years. Her grandparents' desire was for Margaret to be educated. They managed to send her to a girls school where she learned proper use of English and became an excellent speller. She said the girls marveled at how tall she was. She worked in Manchester textile mills a number of years.

Grandmother Agnes Marsden Tindale passed away so it became a responsibility for the pre-teen to cook and care for Grandfather Tindale. She knit his stockings and made her own clothes plus preparing good meals. Grandfather and his fun loving ways were greatly admired by serious Margaret. It is no wonder she was attracted to the amiable and honest young George Vasey with his wonderful sense of humor. Orphaned young, Margaret relished this happy family association. George, the oldest of eight, was born at Ebberston, England, which is three miles from Brompton. His father was a gardener and singer. It was necessary for his children to work to help feed the family.

Margaret continued her needlework. When she married George Vasey in the big brick Episcopal Church Edifice in Brompton, she had prepared necessities for her dowry. She was 20 and he was 21. Their first home was in Brompton, a tiny village, not far from Scarborough the seaport and ocean, in Yorkshire County. Brompton had dirt streets kept neat and rows of brick houses. The climate was damp and foliage was dense green with flowers growing abundantly in bright profusion. The first seven Vasey children were born and recorded in the church register. George was educated in Scarborough and made a living for the family by working as a miller in Brompton.

George's brother Frank worked at shipping docks and heard the sailors talk of America. He listened and determined to someday see that country. When he had saved enough money he bought passage on a ship destined for New Orleans. On board the ship he met an attractive widow with a small daughter. Fascination turned to love and they were married upon arrival in New Orleans. He had friends in Illinois so they chose to settle there. It wasn't long before 18 year old Dowsland, called D, saved enough money for his passage in 1872. D landed in New York and traveled by foot across country to his brother Frank's home in Illinois. What a journey in a strange frontier! He wrote glowing letters relating opportunities of living in America. Quiet Margaret threw American advertisements into their fireplace.

By the time D had two small sons, he was so disgusted with the Illinois climate that he announced he was going back to England. If his wife wouldn't go he would take the boys and leave. She persuaded him to try Nebraska where her parents were living. They agreed and if he still wanted to go back she would go with him and their sons.

In 1883, George and his wife and children left England on the ship MAJESTIC. They wanted a milder climate and the opportunities afforded in America. They brought: Agnes 10, William 9, Hannah 7, Frances 4, Thomas 3, Henrietta 2, and Frank 9 months. Personal belongings were limited to necessities: clothing, bedding, linens and towels. A small mahogany veneer letter box made by Grandfather Tindale and a small silver spoon for baby Frank's teething were packed. Margaret made their clothing and stitched decorations on towels and linens. English royalty had rules restricting what they could take out of the country so they had to choose carefully.

Traveling with George and Margaret and children were his 60 year old parents, Thomas and Hannah Dowsland Vasey; his brothers, John and Tom and sisters, Libby (Elizabeth) and Polly (Mary Ann.) Polly turned down an invitation to be a Lady in Waiting for Queen Victoria for the opportunity to sail to America. Her mistress asked if she planned to go to America when she resigned her position and was disapproving when Polly answered, "Very likely." The trip was long, over rough Atlantic Ocean waters. There was sea sickness and Etta was thought to have died. There was talk of tossing her small body over. She said she was a frail child with a strong constitution. The ship landed on Ellis Island April 22, 1883, on Frances' fifth birthday with Etta still on board.

What an undertaking to give up security of a job and to travel thousands of miles to a strange country not knowing how they would support their family. Courage and confidence were great assets. George and his father had to sign a proclamation denouncing the King of England for U.S. Citizenship. The parents decided to come with the family partly to separate 16 year old Libby from a boyfriend they objected. "It is not known why they objected, he was nice," Elsie wrote. It didn't work. James Langdale followed and they married in New York where they lived for several years.

The Vaseys, except Polly and husband Dave Akers, moved to Eastern Nebraska. The Akers remained in Illinois where Polly looked after little Hanna's grave. Hannah died shortly after they arrived in America. The family settled in Gage County near Blue Springs not far from Beatrice for six years. Janie and her husband, Tom Jenkinson moved to Oklahoma. George and Margaret bought property in Harlan County, southwest of Alma, in 1889 were they lived for the next 26 years before moving into town.

Wash day with huge pots of boiling water was a problem. George and Margaret sat the children on a bench to be certain they were not underfoot when they poured boiling water into the galvanized wash tubs. Etta, at three, said she spotted a lost red rubber ball under the stove as hot water was poured. Quick as a flash she ran to retrieve the ball. She was splashed by the water leaving a scar on her head that she carried all her life.

Father George bought cotton material by the bolt. Margaret sewed dresses and shirts, alike except for decorations and the pattern variations. One time they were all red with white embroidery. The Vasey daughters sewed clothes under Margaret's careful guidance and they sewed for each other. Etta said she made wedding dresses for her sisters, Estella and Frances and herself. They taught their children and grandchildren to sew and properly use a thimble. Margaret spent long evenings knitting socks and toys for her children. Dolls were knit or crocheted from ecru yarn. These made soft lovable toys.

George, as head of the family, was firm and respected. Rarely anyone had to be punished. A word from Father was all that was needed. Youthful children referred seeing an 'old man' and Father told them they were to say Mr. or Mrs. but never 'old.' The children were taught to call their parents "Mother" and "Father."

In 1904, Oliver, 16, suffered a severe stomachache. He walked outside and crawled into a straw stack near their home where he died of a ruptured appendix. Times were hard but with George's optimistic jolly ways and Margaret's positive attitude, they prevailed. The family prospered with hard work and determination setting an example for their descendants.

There is a longing to return when you leave a childhood home. That dream became reality for Margaret and George. They worked and saved until they could make a trip "back home" to visit. Their Harlan County home on an acreage was small but their first crop of oats was good. They were on their way in the "land of opportunity." George bought surrounding acres until he owned his own farm, which he worked with two tamed horses. He added livestock. His sons grew and helped. Finally, George he had enough to afford to take his wife to England to visit in 1907. George, Margaret, Frank and Mary, Dowsland and John returned on an ocean liner. Friends and George's aunts, Fanny and Bess, in England marveled that George owned 300 acres of land. The couple enjoyed the trip but Margaret's letters home showed her thoughts were focused on her children in Nebraska. A neighbor convinced Margaret she should not leave Ruth, the youngest at nine, with the rest of the family. Ruth was to stay with her married sister Frances. Frank took Ruth to Frances' home but on the way he convinced her to return with him. She fared fine at home with her brothers and sisters.

Many changes had taken place in the 24 years since the Vaseys left England. Margaret was sad to see the old Brompton Castle lay in ruins; landmarks and dear friends were sadly missed. Margaret wrote letters to her family often. Frances and Etta kept their letters among treasured keepsakes. The letters they kept were shared for researching their story with the notation, 'Please return.'

George and Margaret were ready to return to America at the end of their visit. They were happy to get back to the family in Nebraska. They were thankful they had left England. The Vaseys sailed for home, November 6, 1907, on the S.S OCEANIC with a passenger capacity of 1,500. They brought with them a chest of gifts; Ruth recalled stick candy. Correspondence with relatives in England continued. Margaret was delighted to receive wedding pictures of her twin nephews.

Margaret was a lady and liked pretty hats. Gifts of breast pins from her family were her favorite jewelry. She sent her children to bed before dark to have time to relax. The young ones who weren't sleepy played quiet games. They'd say, "I'm thinking of a family." Then list the members and change to keep the game going. The Vasey home was five miles southwest of Alma. George had a one horse buggy with shafts that was used to make the trip with either Bird or Nan, his horses. He loved to take grandchildren on rides with him. He doctored sick animals and offered suggestions for sick children. He built a fine home with running water and electric lights. They raised up to 200 hogs and 100 head of cattle along with farm crops. He was voted justice of the peace, chairman of the Eldorado township board and served on the local school board.

Many Vasey descendants inherited the good natured jovial ways of George. Work was made fun by gaiety. Beds were warm and fluffy by stuffed mattress ticks with carefully selected corn shucks or fresh straw. The children did their part to help, all completed 8th grade. Agnes worked as a companion housekeeper for Miss Page and her father in Blue Springs. Frances and Cora became country school teachers. Frances began teaching when the board decided she could teach after 8th grade. She continued for seven years, taking more education at the Orleans Academy. Cora taught several years until her marriage. Etta worked as a midwife and nurse for new mothers and babies. Max went to work for Uncle Frank on his farm. William worked for the Wyoming Railroad. Walter began farming the Noren place and continued farming after his marriage. Frank and Max attended business school. Frank worked as an overseer in the Carbine Coal Mines and was County Treasurer in New Castle, Wyoming for a term or two. Ruth worked for the telephone office in Alma.

Grandfather nicknamed most or all his children, Henrietta was Hettie and Etta, Frank was Boss. Essie was Lady, Walter was Sonny, Albert was Bobby, Ruth was Bairn (Scotch for Baby.)

Max married an older woman who had Tuberculosis. Within a short while he had caught the disease which was fatal in two years, in 1915. He was 35.

The Vasey home was a comfortable wood frame. Margaret had a small bright sitting room with a carpet over straw. The company sitting room was more formal. She loved flowers and kept a pretty yard. She raised petunias, elephant ears, begonias, canna and vines on the farm. She continued crocheting making beautiful edging for towels, scarves and hankies. She made cushion covers and chair 'tidies.' Her clock sat on a shelf and struck the hour. She made quilts and spreads but didn't care for cats, though she fed them.

George was the first in their community to own a cream separator. Soon others saw the advantage and bought one. George was the first to buy a car. His was a Model T Ford touring car. He was pleased with the shiny beauty with brass on the radiator and lamps. He called his car "Sweet lips." His friends laughed. The first time he drove, Margaret sat in the back with her basket of eggs to allow him plenty of space. He started out fine but the narrow road between the corn rows was too much. Before he could get the car going straight, he turned too far and they were bumping over freshly listed corn. Albert, working in the field, noticed his parents' problem so he put up his team and drove them to town. George was glad his neighbors didn't see him and the new Ford in his cornfield! Soon neighbors began driving the country roads with their own shiny black Fords.

Margaret raised turkeys to earn money for a stove. There was much teasing which she took seriously. George and Margaret loved their children and were devoted to all their 29 grandchildren. Margaret wondered at how tall her granddaughters were growing and talked of the girls in school thinking she was so tall at 5' 4". When they gathered at the county fair or Orleans Old Settler's Picnic, George gathered the grandchildren and bought tickets for rides. It was fun for him and for them. He kept a supply of candy in his big desk for every child he met. He bought Jane, an easy going, burro for his grandchildren to ride. The gentle creature couldn't be coaxed to go faster than a slow walk and the children loved riding her. Grandfather and Uncle D, boosted Grandmother on Jane who laughing protested. She was photographed on the back of Jane the burro

Grandfather was warm hearted, friendly and fun loving. When the Vasey families gathered, the house rollicked with happy laughter. There was much joking and horseplay between him and his family. After the children were bedded down in evenings the adults drank tea in the kitchen joking and laughing.

George had confidence that he was welcome anywhere—and he was. After a trip to Lincoln, George remarked to his wife, "I stopped to see 'Brother Charlie.'" (Governor Bryon,) Grandmother exclaimed in horrified tones, "In those clothes!" She was much more reticent.

The farm became too much so George and Margaret moved to Alma and turned the operation to Albert. Moving day, March 6, 1918, dawned bright and clear with much work to be done. Neighbors came to help load wagons, pulled by strong horses and the Vaseys were on their way. Later, Frances, who was widowed, moved her children and livestock to the farm home and worked in partnership with Albert. The house in town was nice with a furnace in the basement and an icebox on the porch. Trees grew in the back yard. Grandchildren would swing on the big double swing hung by chains on the porch. The old striking clock, oblong family picture and sewing machine were among items moved.

Once Grandfather threw coins starting the cousins running to the store for ice cream and candy. When he ran out of nickels and dimes he gave Mildred 50 cents. She took off but was stopped short, that was too much money for a country child.

A trap door to the basement was between the bedrooms in town. Margaret hurried into the closet, only to drop through the trap door which was open for some unknown reason. A bone in her food was broke. She sewed a patch in her shoe to allow for the enlarged bone. The trap door was kept securely closed ever after.

On Sundays Grandfather took the grandchildren to Sunday School. A colored lady speaking, stuck in the memory of some when she said, "I lubs you all." Grandmother stayed home preparing lunch. Boiled meals were common with plenty of puddings. The family sat on benches beside their table; Grandfather filled the plates to serve. Because of her lameness, Grandmother and Elsie walked slowly to church in the evenings. Elsie sat quietly beside

Grandmother. Other young girls whispered and giggled up front, much to grandmother's disapproval.

Christmas Day, 1921 George and Margaret celebrated their 50th Wedding Anniversary. They chose a family affair in their home with family members who could come. The event was the first known of any Vasey and was reported in the local newspaper. It was New Years and summer until all family members were able to share in celebrating.

During school of 1920s, granddaughters stayed with the Vasey grandparents to attend high school. Elsie and Irene loved their grandparents happy ways. They remembered twilight hours with Grandmother crocheting and visiting. Irene said, "When I started high school I had four grandparents in Alma, by the time I graduated in 1928, I had none." They had completed their earthly voyage and were headed to their heavenly mansions.

VASEY GENERATIONS

Francis Dowsland, grandfather of George Vasey, was born October 26, 1859 in England and is buried at Wykhem, England. I saw his tombstone in Wykhem which said he was 72 years old. D's granddaughter, Caroline Rosemon confirmed he was Grandfather of George Vasey. Also located a 'Joseph Vasey, otherwise Vesci,' buried at Wykehem in 1400s, relationship unknown.

Thomas Vasey, was born November. 23, 1822, and married Hannah Dowsland Vasey, born October 17, 1822 and died September 3, 1888. He died July 1,1894. They are buried in the Breathern Cemetery at Holmsville, Nebraska. Some of Dowsland's descendants drove to the Vasey reunion participants to this cemetery a few years ago.

VASEY CHILDREN

William Vasey was born November 23, 1842 in England and died in childhood at six years.

Jane Vasey was born July 22, 1846 and married Tom Jenkinson living in Magnum, Oklahoma.

George Vasey was born January 21, 1849 in Ebberston, England and died December 18, 1926. He married Margaret Tindale, on December 23, 1871 in Brompton, England. She died June 24, 1925. Both are buried in Alma.

Frank Vasey was born March 27, 1851. He married Mary Dutchborn. He died December 28, 1929, in Beatrice, Nebraska.

Dowsland Vasey was born December 6, 1854 and died May 12, 1944. He married Flora Lavina (Sis) Hadley who died on April 1941 at age 85, 12 children-ten boys and two girls were born to them at Liberty, Nebraska.

Mary Ann (Polly) was born January 21, 1857. She wed David Akers, both are buried in Illinois. He died May 10, 1941.

John Vasey was born January 1859 and married Jane Hadley. He died June 25, 1954. They are buried in Tucson, Arizona.

Elizabeth (Libby) was born January 25, 1864 and died May 14, 1941. She married James Langdale, who was born June 9, 1863 and died Aug 4, 1951. They are buried in Beatrice.

Thomas Vasey was born January 9, 1867 and died November 11, 1949. He married Delia Jones and is buried in the Welsh cemetery south of Wymore, Nebraska.

Margaret Tindale, daughter of George Tindale and Agnes Marsden Tindale was born in Manchester, England. She and George Vasey were married in the big church in Brompton. Her grandparents were William and Agnes Tindale who lived in Brompton where he was grounds keeper for a large castle on a hill on the south edge of Brompton. She wrote, she was sad to see the old castle in ruins when they returned. *Our direct ancestors are underlined.

*The Tindale Vasey story is as near as I could reconstruct what I heard through the years of our Vasey ancestors from Grandma Etta Vasey Paine. I wrote many letters and made numerous phone calls asking multitudes of questions to gather this information. My mother took a tape recorder to the nursing home to record Grandma's answers to more questions. Grandma recalled details and laughed at family antics while repeating stories. Her laughter made me laugh with her. I played the tape until it broke.

*This research was a labor of love for my family, my mother, my grandma and our extended Vasey cousins. Frances and Etta shared their letters for gleaning information. I walked inside and out the impressive big Brompton church to take pictures and look. Daphne Vasey of Ebberston shared her family records back to 1680 that matched our family records. She called the church rector to ask permission for me to walk in the Ebberston Church where Thomas and Hannah Dowsland Vasey were married. Vasey tombstones were everywhere.

IMOGENE AND THE TRAVELING TRUNK

"Imogene!" called Peter Shafer to his daughter. "Come see the trunk. You may have this trunk for your very own packing."

"Oh, thank you Papa," exclaimed the child. She quickly knelt down beside the trunk to trace her fingers over the brass copper tacks that spelled the letters P.S. on the black furry leather hide covered the wooden trunk. This was her father's favorite trunk. It was small and handy to take and perfect for a little girl's clothes and treasures.

In 1855 the family, Ann Eliza Paine Shafer, her husband Peter, a school teacher and their daughter, Imogene, were preparing for a trip by covered wagon from New York to Illinois. Imogene was born March 26, 1850 at Sidney Plains, near Sanford, Delaware County, New York. The family planned to go farther west where teachers were needed. Ann Eliza had relatives transplanted to Illinois so the trip was happily anticipated.

Imogene wore her long hair pulled back in braids and high topped shoes under her new dark ankle length dress. Her mother made the dress with high collar and wrist length sleeves and a new bonnet for the trip.

Imogene skipped with excitement, she was not sleepy because of many thoughts racing through her active mind. "Tell me again, Mother," she pleaded, "about your grandfather." Thus, Ann Eliza, a woman of 33, began relating stories she had heard of her ancestors. "Grandfather was Seth Paine," she began. "It is believed that he came to America with his cousin, Thomas Paine and another cousin on a ship." Grandfather was a judge in New York." "Were you there then?" innocently asked little Imogene.

Ann Eliza patiently explained to her daughter. "No, I was born May 18, 1822. My Grandfather was a judge during the 1770s." "Grandfather Paine had several sons. My father was Abijah. Ephraim and Sally, who married Mr. Boyd, were his siblings.

"Grandmother was Mary Elizabeth Babcock Paine, called Betsy, who died young. He later married a lady named Annis.

Ephraim's wife was a Livingston. They had a daughter named Eliza Paine Crandall."

Imogene drifted to sleep. Ann Eliza continued thoughts of her family as she busied herself packing. She had prepared food, clothing and several favorite chairs. The last items to add were personal papers she sorted to keep. 'We will miss sister Harriet and brother George in New York. We could see them on holidays but they will be far away. It will be wonderful to see brother Fulwar and Mary and families who left Illinois.'

Ann Eliza thought, 'Here is the letter I wrote to Harriet when Imogene was born.' She began reading: "Stanford, April 13, 1850 Dear Sister, I have felt for a long time that I ought to write to you and let you know how I am getting along. I cannot write much at present for I have a lot of trouble on my hands in the shape of a little girl, who is now about three weeks old- Everybody says that she is a very fine baby, although she's rather cross. I am writing now with the paper on the arm of my rocking chair and the babe on my lap- We are living with Mr. Bothrick but intend moving on our own place week after next. Mrs Bothrick is a sister of Mr. Brownell, they are strong Methodists, yet we like them very much.

Emily wrote that Richard has become pious. I was glad to hear the news for I thought you would enjoy yourself better. I expected you and Richard would make us a visit last winter but was sadly disappointed. I hope you will come this summer or fall. We calculate to make you a visit in the course of summer. I have received a letter from Mary which I shall enclose... You must write her....give my love to Mary, Nelson and to Mr. Hilton's family also to Mr. Green's people. I am quite smart. Peter's health is very good. I cannot write any more so I will bid you "Good Bye. Eliza" Sent to Mrs. Harriet Haughtalling of North Franklin Delaware County, New York.

Ann Eliza continued, Sister Mary, the oldest, was born in 1804. She and Nelson have been in Illinois since 1836. The years go by quickly. Their son Henry was born in 1837; he would be 18 now. Brother Fulwar Skepwith is in Chicago. I understand he is a good doctor. He married Mary Orton Hoit, September 23, 1841. She is younger, a likable sister-in-law; they have: George Franklin, Cassius, Albert, Lois Marie, and Fulwar.

Brother Fulwar's 1845 letter: "Dear Sister, The delay in answering your letter is so inexcusable it is not worthwhile to make comment. It was some months before I rec'd it being directed to the wrong office, I handed it to sister Mary. She thought she would answer it so that you might come this spring but she failed to do so on account of the intemperate habits of her husband which she had hoped would get better but of late seem to be on the increase. She would liked to have you come live with her but thought it would not be agreeable to you to live where whiskey now wont to be used with regard to you coming. I could not tell you what would be the prospect of millinery business in the towns yet think there is enough for all purposes that follow the trade I have a pleasant farm on the property in a good neighborhood which I bought since I wrote home last. You would find hire work enough in millinery dress making and garments. My wife when young followed this business and can make a better coat than a tailor to the price for such work which are higher than when they were when I left New York. If you do not find yourself comfortable and agreeably situated in down north should you come this way you would meet with a cordial welcome.

Mrs. Paine is anxious you should come live with us…she would give you in instruction in sewing when we get a new house build which I hope will not be many years we could make you as comfortable as you would find. She is a warm hearted and generous woman provided a little family scolding did not scare you. Travel would be Buffalo by water to Chicago, stage to Rockford then private convoy to Gyles. The price from Buffalo to Chicago for cabin passage is eight or ten dollars. You should plan by mid September to ensure a pleasant passage…We want to hear from Davenport and how you all prosper…. There is prospects of great crops of wheat, corn, and oats…at a fair price. Your affectionate Brother, FS Paine"

Ann Eliza continued sorting, The Hoit family traces family history back to Simon Hoit in colonial records who descended from Baron Von Haight who traveled from Normandy to Britain in the 13th century. Family records quoted say, "The American branch of the family trace ancestry to that sterling puritan Simon Haught born in Dorsetshire, England, in 1595 and sailed to America October 6, 1628, on the vessel Abigail with Col. John Endicott who afterward was appointed governor of Massachusetts Colony."

Simon Haight brought with him his wife and sons, John, Walter and Nicholas. He settled at Salem and later moved to Stamford, Connecticut where he died on September 1,1651. Some descendants live in Connecticut. Simon Hoit was one of the first settlers of Dorchester, Massachusetts as his name appears in 1635. By then he moved to Scituate, Massachusetts where he and his wife joined a church in April. They went to Windsor, Connecticut where he is in land records in 1640. Nicholas, was born about 1624. He married in 1646 and died in 1655. Nicholas' son, Johnathan was born in Windsor June 7, 1649 and by 1672, he was at Gifford, Connecticut. He received allotments of land, 70 acres for him 40 for his wife and 40 for each of the children.

Peter, Ann Eliza and Imogene lived in Rockford, Illinois for ten years. Imogene grew to be an intelligent, quiet young woman. When she was 15 she attended a whistle stop meeting for the campaigning Abraham Lincoln. Imogene was fortunate, being of small stature, to stand in front when Mr. Lincoln stepped down to shake hands with the people, the people he was elected to serve as president of the US the following year. It was a thrill for Imogene and her parents to reminisce the meeting. Petite Imogene remained interested in politics the rest of her life. She shook hands with the president and resolved to study and keep abreast of news.

The West was developing and Peter was interested in securing land for himself in southern Nebraska or Kansas. The trip would be difficult. It was decided Imogene, now 21, and called Gene, would travel with her father. Mother and Grandmother could come later.

Imogene wrote her mother often but mostly her letters recorded uneventful days of traveling, good weather and distance covered. The wagon was pulled by mules and a horse, named Kitty. They traveled alone until they met a group of emigrants heading for Kansas.

The little trunk was cared for and it made the journey west with it's young owner. It was useful though the contents were now fitting of a young lady. Then came a letter to Ann Eliza dated Beatrice, Nebraska, Thursday, October. 5, 1871: "Dear mother, I hardly know how to commence my letter for I have bad news to write. We have met with quite an accident. Yesterday while father was walking beside the wagon his foot slipped into a rut. The wagon ran over and broke his leg, just above the ankle. We are seven miles from here. We have taken a part of a house and moved in right away. His leg was set as soon as we arrived and seems to be doing well. He made friends with the Masonic Fraternity and we have all the assistance we need. Of course, we would like to have you and Grandma come as soon as you conveniently can. I will write to you again in a day or two with directions how to come and where to send the goods. Do not start until you get it and after that as soon as you want to. Do not be uneasy if you cannot get ready to come under a fortnight for we are as comfortable as we could possibly be under the circumstances. Rents are dear but everything else is cheaper than in Picatonica. Father has hope of getting work on the rail road that is being built here for it is probable we shall have to stay this winter now, but we can talk that all over when you come. We will send directions about the leg in the next letter and I wish you will answer this. Be sure and do not start until you hear from us again. Give my love to Auntie, Mrs. Coffin and to all. Gene"

Ann Eliza came to Beatrice where Peter served as a judge for two years,1877 to 1879. He worked primarily as a school teacher. Imogene, now known as Gene, took a job as one of the first Beatrice librarians. After several years she resigned the library job to take a position as type-setter for The Beatrice Sun, an early newspaper,. She worked at this position for years and was faster than most. She was a printer, and compositor in hand type days. Her rating was 'swift.' The Beatrice Sun reported, "When machines made hand setting obsolete, she mastered the lino type and continued her trade."

Cassius grew and began courting blue eyed Minerva Covell. Her diary kept daily at the time, records many entries, "Cassius was here." Then came a separation and Cassius wrote Minerva a letter which she'd saved: "Auburn, September. 2, 1865, Dear Nerva, I take this opportunity to write you a few lines for the first time in my life. The folks are all well here at present excepting me and all that ails me is because I am so lonesome. Times are rather dull here for company it seems as if everybody had left. I have not seen Blue since you left but I guess she is all right. Pert says she is going out to get two or three girls to stay here for company. They had a big dance at Sam Berry's and the same night you left so they say. I was not up there. Sunday the 3, Nerve, I will write you a few more lines and then draw to a close. Hatty Thornton has been staying here for three or four days. She went to see Mr. Lees this morning. She is bound to stay in the country I guess. She does not love a city life very well. Nerve, I have not got that picture taken yet but will as soon as I can get time. I have not had time to go anywhere yet. They are going to have a dance up to Gooslsberg next Friday night. Pert is going with Darwin Berry, I suppose. Mr. Eastman is buying up cows he bought one yesterday and two today. He swears he will have cows enough and the best news of all is Cander Lee has a boy. I do not know whether it drools any yet. This is all for this time. Write soon. Excuse bad writing. I wrote this up stairs on the bed. It does not look fit to send away but it is hard work for me to write so I will send it. From your affectionate friend, C. M. Paine"

Friendship blossomed and an entry in Minerva's diary on November 30, 1865, says "Cassius got married." The wedding ceremony took place in Lyonsville County, Illinois by Rev James Vial. Cassius was a young man of 20 and his bride was 22.

Time rolled on for Gene and her relatives. Cousin Cassius began farming and raised four children: Mertie in 1867, Charlie in 1870, Maud in 1875 and Claude in 1881. Maud was a sickly one. Communication was more infrequent as the cousins were busy making a living.
In the spring of 1899 Cassius dictated a letter to Mertie to write to his cousin Gene to thank her for material she had mailed. He told her family news and of relatives then he thanked her properly. He wrote, "I thank you very much for the papers you sent me, and as they are mostly Populist papers so much the better, for me at least. You say you are populist, so we can not quarrel at that point and if we quarrel at all it will have to be about something else." He offered a warm welcome if she would visit him and his family.

Years took a toll on the Paine family. Gene was living alone in Beatrice at 80. She was fond of Charlie's wife, Fannie who was widowed young. It was agreed that Fannie would move to Beatrice to care for Gene in her final years. Fannie had grown children: Elsie, Nell and Howard. It was refreshing to have them stop by. They were thoughtful young people. Fannie and Charlie lost their first, Edith a much loved little girl with golden curls, at three.

Patriotic duties were still a priority for Gene, Elsie remembered. "One time" she wrote, "when Gene was in her 80s, she and Mother were on their way to vote when they were given a ride by a business man. She gave him such a convincing talk about the duty of citizens vote that he went home, got his wife and they voted, which they had not planned on doing."

Gene was a quiet, sensible lady. She was interested current events. Fannie reported Gene sat up all night listening to a presidential convention on the radio. She loved to read and continued despite failing eyesight. Gene lived independently riding her bicycle to town for years. If she needed food for her pet cat, or dry bread to feed birds in the yard, whatever the weather, she set out downtown some blocks away.

At 97, Gene met extended family, Cassius's youngest son, Claude's grandchildren, Lila, Jim, Beth, Ted, Glen and Gene plus Charlie's granddaughter Joan came to shake her hand. She seemed so petite. She preferred not having her picture taken but was gracious. Fannie brought a dish of strawberries and Gene said, "Those were good tomatoes." Age dimmed her taste and her vision but not her manners.

On March 26, 1950, Gene celebrated her 100th birthday. The Beatrice Times put her picture and story on the front page. Businesses sent bouquets of flowers and boxes of fruit to her home. Miss Shafer received cards from President, Harry S. Truman and the Nebraska senators, making it a day to remember. Months later, Gene was hospitalized where she quietly passed away. She had lived a successful life, spanning terms of twenty-one presidents, from Zachary Taylor to Harry S. Truman. Imogene Shafer came to end of a long life. The little trunk was passed to another generation.

HERITAGE

Our mother taught us to write thank you letters the day after we received gifts. Elsie sent Christmas gifts every year. We were appreciative and worked hard on notes to her. In this age of instant gratification many never write thank you notes or letters. They do not know what they are missing. To communicate in a letter is great way to make contact. I had letters written by ancestors years ago. I find them interesting. I've learned family facts by reading old letters. A letter addressed to Cassius and Minerva dated, February 15, 1900, begins: "As you say, Cassius writing is a slow way of talking. All the meaning of a word seems to ooze out before it can be written down. I was glad to get your pictures. You have got a fine face Cassius but you look more like my own Father than yours as I remember him. I was not 14 years old when he left for the west. Yet, I can see him still as he bade me good bye and gave me good counsel, I know I went out to the stable where his horse had been kept and cried myself sick. How do you manage Minerva to keep such a cheerful and Jolly face up into the fifties? It did me good to see it. But won't you send me a larger one bye and bye. A large one of all your family. I shall send you mine but it is a poor old grumpy toothless thing as you will see. Mertie wrote that you would like to know more about your kins people on the Paine side. Well I can't tell you much of the present generation for I have lost track of them for which I am very sorry. You see what comes of being a bad correspondent. But I console myself with the thought that they will not mind it as much. The younger fry were getting to stylish to relish our old fashioned ways. Come see us when it comes pleasant weather and I will tell you about your Great Grandfather for you really have one who was famous and rich in his day. And who besides being Judge and Senator and Congressman were also cousin to Poor old Tom Paine whose name is used to frighten naughty children. Henry Salisbury got 40 dollars an acre for his farm which will make a tidy sum for his old age. Well I must bid good bye. I hope you can read this, Eliza Shafer"

Ann Eliza Shafer, younger sister to Cassius Paine's father, Dr. Fulwar Skipwith Paine was born in 1805. She wrote to my great grandparents. The Doctor's father was Obijah Paine, a statesman according to family records. Fulwar married Mary Orton Hoit on September 15, 1841. He earned a medical degree from Rockford, Illinois. I once saw a letter written by Dr. Fulwar stating he was thinking of buying a farm, "It would be a more sure income than medicine." I saw his black medical bag hid away in a closet when I was little. I asked my mother about the stethoscope and various assorted tubes of colored medicines. She said it had belonged to her great grandfather and contained medicine. She moved the bag and I never saw it again. My brother, Gene said he remembered seeing the black medical bag but we couldn't find it when we searched.

The Shafer family traveled by horse and buggy from Illinois to Beatrice in the 1800s. They were headed to Kansas but stopped in Beatrice because of the accident. Imogene Shafer wrote telling of trials on the trail. Her faded old letters are how I learned. Family heirlooms, like her lamp, dishes, tintype pictures, letters, postcards, and scissors came from Imogene Shafer and were stolen the spring of April 2009. There was a huge roll top trunk full of old clothes, letters, patterns and much more. A part of our family history is gone. There are few letters and pictures which reflect our family heritage. I am thankful my family is safe. We can share heritage memories. *Letters from cousins, and friends were addressed to "Sister Nerva, Cousin Nerva or Nellie." I inherited these letters when my Dad said, "I don't know what to do with this shoe box of letters; maybe they should be burned." "No!" I exclaimed, "I will take them if you don't want them." Suggestions for preserving this bit of history are welcome.

PAINE FAMILY RECORD

Last Name	First Name	Office Held	Year
Paine	Abijah	Supervisor	1835
Paine	Abijah	Supervisor	1836
Paine	Abijah	Overseer of Highways	1836
Paine	Abijah	Overseer of Highways	1841
Paine	Abijah	Overseer of Highways	1846
Paine	Abijah	Assessor	1851
Paine	Abijah	Assessor	1852

Marriages - 1846 - 1853 Delaware County New York

Denend, Esq., Peter SHAFER of Baskenridge, New Jersey to Ann Eliza PAINE daughter of Abijah of Davenport. May 2, 1849 Walton 26th ult. ww.dcnyhistory.org/oldnewsidx/kitty3.html 15th inst., by E.Denend,Esq., Peter SHAFER of Baskenridge, New Jersey to Ann Eliza PAINE daughter of Abijah Paine of Davenport May 2, 1849 Gage County

Beatrice Census 1880	Name & homestead number
Imogene SHAFER	6013
Shaffer Eliza	w f 58 Beatrice
Shaffer Imogene	w f 30 Beatrice
Shaffer Peter	w m 60 Beatrice

CIVIL WAR NEWS

Training Station Georgia July 2,1865

Dear Sister,

    Today I snatch a few moments to pen you a few lines for <u>the</u> express purpose of telling you the <u>news.</u>, but not with the hope of being the first one to tell you what I am going to tell you because I am well aware that the telegraph news travel faster then news by mail, so therefore I write to confirm the news you have already received, VIZ, Atlanta Georgia has fallen. The Fourth Corps entered the city this morning, so far all is well for Johnson's Army is demoralized and retreating to the south west. I hear Sherman is in full pursuit. I feel certain the Rebel Army is a thing of the past in this part of the country known for the last three years as "Dixie." Where the Rebels will make their next stand is now conjectun (sic) on my part, but I guess somewhere between here and the Gulf of Mexico.

    There was a heavy fight day before yesterday in which the Rebels got the worst of the bargain but we lost a good many good men. I can't tell how many because I have not yet learned, but in a gigantic Campaign like this it must be expected that we will lose some men. I hardly think the campaign will end with the capture of Atlanta for Sherman is not the ma to say "let's stop I'm tired of chasing Johnson" but he will follow him Mobile if he goes therein.

    Well almost enough about Sherman so I will say a word about Grant and company. If Grand can take Richmond then the rest will be easy in comparison to the taking of Atlanta and Richmond How did the Rebels make out in their raid into Maryland? I think they were rather glad to get away from that place but they got a great deal of plan and I should think by the accounts the papers give of the raid I forgot to tell you I have a view of Atlanta in the distance. It is seven milers from here to there.

    I wrote a letter to Mrs. Payne two or three days ago telling her that her son was very sick and so I told her I thought he could not live. When I saw him I asked him if he thought he would ever get well. and he told me he thought he would have a hard time of it if he did get well. I asked him if he had anything he wanted to send to his mother.& he told me that he lost all the things he had in the Division Hospital so he had nothing to give me. He was sent to Chattanooga when he left Marietta and died on the way there he was buried at Trundle Hill by the Regt garrisoning the Post. I think we will soon move on to Atlanta and establish the hospital there as soon as we get there and I will write and tell you. I have got to get back this morning so if I go tonight I shall not get back until morning again. I hope I shall get a letter from you. This time for I can't tell when it was I got my last letter from you but it was some time in April or May. well at most I can't get many more letters from you or anyone else, when you write tell me all the news. I have no news for so long I begin to think there is no news I think I told Ellen I saw William Bryan. They were both well then give my love to Father and Mrs. Wright (sounds green don't it) Charles and William and Joseph tell him that latter. So I will close for this time. With much love I am the same as ever.

       Your True, Brother Albert Barsby

CIVIL WAR LETTER

This gleaning came from a letter written in the 1860s from my great grandmother, Minerva Paine's brother, Marcellus J. Covell to his family during the Civil War. Marcellus tells about intense fighting. There isn't a date but he writes, "Tell Mary that I do not wear woolen in the southern climate and am forever obliged to her for the kind offer." He wonders if his friend in "R" is pretending to be tongue tied until the Draft is over because he hasn't heard from him.

He writes, "I must ask if they see sister Mariah?" He requests they tell her to write. He continues: "I feel that a sister that was once such a kind and tender sister should forget a brother just because he is a soldier in the defense of her home and fireside. It grieves me to the heart and I shed a tear as I right (sic) these few lines. If you tell her she has my best wishes and shall have whilst I live and her children also.

"The enemy are coming into our lines daily and giving themselves up as deserters saying there is no will of fighting longer. A few days since a rebel Col. came in and gave himself up and went to Memphis and took the Oath.

"The regt. had an election for the president and they all voted for Old Honest Abe with very few exceptions and they voted for McClellan. I do not think that this war is to last a great many years longer and I might say months.

"If anyone asks how the soldiers are here in this Calv. Division tell them they are for the war to the bitter end and we are not tired of the war until we are victorious. Since I have been sitting here I have heard artillery firing in the distance. It may be a fight with our patrol that went out early this morning. We may have to go soon to reinforce them before I write you this. From MJC" (Marcellus J. Covell)

(Later Marcellus was killed in a battle in the south after being sick in a hospital several times. Their sister Marcella (Lettie) joined the service as a nurse to find her brother. He tells in one letter of finding her in a hospital when she was very ill. She survived to an old age and continued a daring outgoing person. His diary and old letters are evidence of an honest, determined young soldier thinking of his family and friends who loved him. There were eight in the family and all their names began with M.)

MOMS WRITING

The Paine family moved in 1913 from Oxford to Stapleton, the place later became 'The Lariat Boys Ranch.' Claude and Etta bought the Ed Carter land in 1916 and moved by covered wagon, hay rack and a saddle horse with their collie dog, driving a small herd of cattle to Cherry County, arriving in December. Claude and Etta took over the Elizabeth Post Office, named for the Uehling's daughter, Elizabeth. The Post Office was discontinued in 1931 when a mail route was established to carry mail to and from Wood Lake, 25 miles north on trail roads.

The Paine's didn't move but their address was Elizabeth, Elsmere, Wood Lake and now mail is delivered from Valentine. The Paine family lived in a sod house which was cozy warm in winter and comfortably cool in summer. Claude Seth Paine was born April 6, 1881 near Oxford, Nebraska. He married on March 16, 1908, to Henrietta Ellen (Etta) Vasey, daughter of George and Margaret Tindale Vasey in Alma, Nebraska. They trace ancestors to England.

Her mother, Margaret lived with her Tindale grandparents in an old castle at the edge of Brompton on the northern coast of England. Their ancestry is traced to William Tindale, who was burned at stake for his translation of the King James Version of the Bible into English.

Claude and Etta had Irene and Mildred who attended country school in District # 102. Irene graduated from Alma High School in 1928, staying with her Vasey grandparents. Mildred graduated from Curtis High in 1941. Both taught rural schools in Cherry County. Mildred married Sgt. Thomas S. Wagenseil and they live in California with Judy, David and Jeanne.

The Paine family has recorded history back to Simon Hoit in Salem, Massachusetts in 1628. Claude's parents were Cassius Marcellus Clay Paine born in Winnebago County, Illinois, on August 16, 1845. Cassius died February 2, 1926 and is buried at Stamford, Nebraska. He married Minerva Covell at Lyonsville, Illinois on November 30, 1865. She was born in Proviso, Illinois on February 28, 1843 and died December 12, 1926 in Alma. They had four children: Mary Maud, Mertie Elizabeth and Charlie Bruce who came to Harlan County, Nebraska in 1878 from Illinois. Claude Seth was born in 1881 in their sod home near the Republican River. Claude's grandparents were Dr. Fulwar S. and Mary Orton Hoit Paine. Great Grandparent, Seth Paine, a judge and senator is said to be a cousin of Thomas Paine, author of Common Sense which changed the tide in Revolutionary War.

Paul and Irene Weber are parents of six children. He ranched and she was a full time mother except the one year she taught her family when Gene was a baby. Her mother cooked and watched Glen and Gene, the youngest. Their family:

Lila and John Ahrens, Lee, Tom, and Joe of Chadron. Lila graduated from Alma High School in 1952 and attended Chadron State College graduating with a BS degree in August 1988. She taught school several years before marriage. (Johnny died of cancer in July 2009. Lila has five grandchildren and four great grandsons.)

James (Jim) and Rebeca, Nick, Chris, Tim and Janel of Purdum. Jim graduated from Thedford High in 1954 and CSC in 1958. He was drafted in the Army and was stationed in Korea. He taught and farmed near Purdum in Blaine County and raised Pinzgauer cattle. He was paralyzed by a horse accident on March 3, 1983, after loosing his hand in a corn picker earlier. (They have eight grandchildren and five great grandchildren.)

Elizabeth (Beth) and Harold Gibbons, Jerry, Wayne and Kristi of Crawford. Beth was a graduate of TCHS in 1955 and taught. Their sons: Jerry Dean and Wayne Harold graduated from Western Technical School in Sidney in Mechanical and Carpentry. Kristi Irene earned a Business degree from Rapid City in May 1992. She earned a Masters Degree in Business and Accounting from CSC. Beth substitute teaches and freelance writes. She graduated from CSC in elementary education. Harold suffered a heart attack at home on May 18,1992. (Beth has 12 grandchildren and four great grandchildren.)

Theodore (Ted) graduated from TCHS in 1958. He was seriously injured in a car accident in early August 1956. He was involved in ranching with his parents for a time. He married Clara and they live at Mission, South Dakota.

Glen and Lauretta, Gary and Glenda of Centennial, Colorado. Glen graduated from TCHS in 1959 and took automotive training in Kansas City. He owns and operates a garage in Evergreen, Colorado. Gary and Glenda have Master's degrees in counseling and in education. (They have six grandchildren.)

Gene Paul, 1961 graduate of TCHS and 1965 graduate of CSC taught in Cody High School before being drafted by the Army in 1968. He took training in Fort Lewis, Washington where he received an honorable medical discharge. He taught again then joined the staff of Weld County Hospital in Greeley, Colorado. He was supervisor for years over near 100 employees. Gene is retired from Weld County Hospital and works for Greeley City parks and volunteers in local schools. Gene never married.

(Update: Paul and Irene celebrated their golden anniversary in 1983 and 60th in 1994, a year late because of Jim in the hospital, at the Halsey Shelter Building with many family and friends. They had two great grandchildren, Kim Renee born July 24, 1978 and Ben John born November 11, 1979. Added Great Grandchildren: Dustin Lee Weber born February 1980; Andrew Paul Gibbons born April 27, 1985; William Scott Gibbons born September 2, 1986; Cody Don Gibbons born July 12, 1987; Joseph Dean Gibbons born July 19, 1988 and died October 31, 1999; Stacie Marie Weber born August 25, 1986; Kayla Andre Weber born December 27, 1987; Ashley Elizabeth Gibbons born January 21, 1992; Coleman John Ahrens born April 27, 1992; Tyler Walker Childs born July 27, 1992; Tanner Michael Childs born July 9, 1994; Tiara Joy Childs born December 23, 1998; Kendra Joy Weber born March 13, 1996; Katelynn Nicole Weber born December 29, 1993; Rachel Grace Weber born July 12, 2001; Ian Carson Ahrens born April 15, 1994; Logan Garret Ahrens born April 11, 1996 and Alyssa Mae Snyder born September 11, 2003; Mindra Oana Lynda Gibbons born July 15, 1993 in Romania; Ana Angelica Gibbons born December 30, 1993 in Romania; Ivan John Gibbons born September 4, 1999 in Russia; Ben Emeil Gibbons born August 27, 2004 in Russia; Marina Grace Gibbons born January 24, 1991 in Donetsk, Estonia and Jade Susu Gibbons born April 2, 2004 in China. Their Great great grandchildren are: Carson Wayne Gibbons born March 7, 2007 in Germany; Joseph Ronald Gibbons born October 31, 2008; Addie Nichole Gibbons born February 27, 2009; Teyton Lee Haas born

April 12, 2008; Jayce John Hass born May 21, 2010; Brayden Syvon Ahrens born December 20. 2009 and Treye Rueger Gibbons born March 10, 2011.)

Early neighbors: Hans and Christina Larsen from Aalborg, Denmark; Theodore and Frances Foitlinski from Germany; Henry and Marjorie Voss, Arlene, Jerry, Darwin, Eldon and Kayo; Floyd and Ella Keller, Josephine, Elmer and Joann; Francis and Helen Gudgel, David, Willard, Duane and Linda; Sherman and Margie Gudgel, Ardith, Arbell, Alice, Steven and Michael; Quinton and Bessie Smith, Harlan and Jeanine; Henry and Mable Voss and Vivian; Charlie and Ella Daniels, Shirley, Edsel and Duane.

Irene was called to heaven, July 9, 1994, at age 85. Services were held in Ainsworth on July 12th, Cody's 7th birthday. Paul passed to meet his Savior, August 5,1996, the day before his 89th birthday. Memorials were in Ainsworth with large turnouts of family and friends expressing caring. We were humbled with the tremendous outpouring of love and respect shown for our parents, their children, grandchildren and great grandchildren.

Young Harold Gibbons enjoying his swing at their rural Crawford home, about 1928.

HAROLD'S STORY
By Harold Gibbons

I was born on a farm about five and three fourth miles South East of Crawford, Nebraska on December 12, 1923. I have lived there all my life which is fifteen years. My Mother and Father and Grandparents are English. My Mother and Father are both from the Eastern part of the state where my father was engaged in farming. He is still a farmer.

The place where I live is by a creek with trees all around. The creek is below the house. It is a very pretty place in the summer along the creek when the grass and trees are green and the flowers are in bloom. In the fall of the year after the leaves have fallen there is good hunting through the timber. The first year of my life there were not many cars and people traveled with horse pulled buggies and spring wagons. The hauling was all done with team and wagons and bob sleds.

I remember very distinctly when a man hauled twenty loads of hogs with bob-sleds when the roads were blocked and they had to travel through our yard. I stood by the window and watched them go by. Before my Father moved to this place there was an old saw mill that was run by a water wheel.

When I was two years old we went to town and other places with a 1918 Maxwell car with side curtains. When I was three years old, we bought a new Ford car.

I remember very well one time there was a very bad hail storm. We had just got back from the neighbors when the storm struck. I was sitting in a high chair eating a chicken leg when the storm started. It broke out quite a lot of the windows out of the house. A lot of the trees were killed in the timber. All the crops were ruined because it happened right at the time of year when the farmers where cutting their grain. This was a great loss even the farmers who had their grain in the shock because the hail pounded it all out. It also cut the corn just like if you had gone over it with a mowing machine. It also knocked the shingles of the West side of the house full of holes and it all had to be re-shingled.

I learned to color and write my name early. My father made a writing desk for me and on stormy days I would color and write. I remember very well the first time I rode a horse because I had my picture taken while I was on the horse.

My father attended school at Walthill, Nebraska until he reached the ninth grade. He then moved with his parents to Crawford, Nebraska and lived on a farm. In two years he decided to go back to school so he went to York, Nebraska where he took business courses for three years. He then came back to Crawford, Nebraska and started farming and is still a farmer. My mother also attended school at Walthill, Nebraska. After she graduated from High School, she worked in the Post Office at Walthill. Later my mother decided to take the Civil Service Examination. Within a month she was appointed as clerk in the Sioux City Post Office. She was chosen money order, postal saving and war saving bond window clerk. She handled many hundreds of dollars each day. This position she held until she was married.

After my Father and Mother were married they lived for one year with my grandparents. The next year they moved on to a place South-East of Crawford where we still live. I have always lived on the place adjoining my Grandmother and Grandfather Gibbons. I have always liked farming and intend to be a farmer when I grow up.

Before I started school my mother taught me to write and do some reading. In the first grade I learned how to read and spell by learning the sounds as they were called. In my first year I had a very good teacher. I also had a good teacher for my second year of school but my third year my teacher didn't take very much interest in teaching us. I didn't get my studies so good that year. For my next three years of school I had a very good teacher. When I was in the fifth grade I lost four weeks of school because of the whooping cough.

I can look back at the happy days that I had in school. When I was in the first, second, and third grade, we would always take toys to school to play with. We had a sand pile where we made caves or cellars and many other things in the ground at recesses and noons. When I was in the fourth, fifth, and sixth grade I rode a horse to school at this time there were between twenty and twenty-five children going to school there.

Sometimes the teacher would take us on hikes which was always a lot of fun. One day a bunch of kids and I decided to play hooky so we ran away and went to the creek. Before four o' clock we came back and the teacher gave us a scolding. When I got home I got a worse scolding from my parents so I never played hooky again.

I was 12 years old when I was in the eighth grade. The eighth grade was the hardest year in grade school. In the country schools you have to take the county examinations which are given in town at the city school house. The teacher will teach you the things that are provided in the course of study. I had to study real hard in order to pass. When I got my examination grades back I found that I had passed with an average of eighty-six percent. On the twentieth of May the eighth graders go to Chadron or Crawford where they receive their diplomas. I received mine at Crawford at the auditorium. The diplomas are handed out by the county superintendent Leora A. Rustin who lives at Chadron and has her office in the court house. The diplomas are given to show that the pupil has completed the course of study for the eight years and is now promoted to go to High School beginning with the ninth grade and continuing on up through the twelfth grade. I was very happy when I received my diploma because I knew that I could go to High School which I had been working for a long time.

The first long trip I remember taking was my Father, Mother and I going to eastern part of the state to a small town where my Grandfather and Grandmother lived. They were my Grandparents on my Mother's side. The name of the town was Walthill, Nebraska where my Mother lived before she was married. My Father had lived near there. We went to Chadron, Nebraska and on down on highway number twenty. We stayed all night at Long Pine where we went to a tourist cabin to spend the night. I remember very well about this trip especially how bad the roads were through the Sandhills before the roads were graveled or oiled.

My father was talking to a man at a filling station and Dad was telling him how bad roads were but the man said they were considered good if you could get through without getting stuck and having to get a team of horses to pull you out.

I have taken three or four trips to Walthill. One was when I was a baby and went by train and I didn't remember much about it. The next to the last time that I went we had bought a new car and drove through in one day. While I was there my aunt took us to Lincoln where we visited the State Capital and other places including the zoo which was interesting because we saw so many different animals from other countries.

I experienced a number of exciting events when riding horseback to school. One morning, on my way to school, I was riding my horse along beside another boy who was also riding a horse. All of a sudden my horse gave a quick jump and I was almost thrown off. I was just hanging to the horses mane to stay on.

Another time I was riding home from school when there was quite a bunch of children walking behind. I was riding down a little hill with my reins loose and not paying much attention to my horse. All of us kids were talking and then one of the small boys in the group decided that he wanted to see my horse run. He picked up a rock and threw it at my horse which frightened her and she gave a quick jump and I fell off right under her heels. Luckily she stopped and I just got one bruise where her hoof had struck my leg.

When riding to school I got lots of thrills. Many times there were four or five of us boys riding along the road at nights and mornings. Our hardest job was to carry our lunch pail. My Mother made a bag with a strap for me to carry mine in so I could put it over my shoulder. At noon we had to feed and water our horses, sometimes we pumped water, and other times we would ride them over to the creek that was only a short distance away.

I passed the eighth grade with an average of eighty-six percent. The day that I came in to sign up for my Freshman year of High School, I didn't know much about town school as I had never gone to school in town.

When I was a freshman I took four subjects: English, algebra and agriculture, which counts as two. I am a sophomore taking subjects this year which are quite a lot harder. They are English III, Geometry and Farm Management. In Geometry a person has to learn all the theorems and rules or else you won't be able to prove the propositions. In English I study effectiveness of speech, word lists and many other interesting things. In Agriculture we work in the shop on Tuesday and Thursday and study in the classroom the other three days of the week. In Farm management we learn how to manage a farm properly. We are now learning how to fill out farm account books which is interesting. We learn how to figure the price that a farmer gets for his cream by multiplying the number of pounds by the percent of butterfat times the price which gives the amount received.

In this biography I have told my history from one year to my present age of 15 years.

My mother, Irene, with the Rose Quilt, I designed and sewed for my parents' 40th Wedding Anniversary in 1973.

EARLY YEARS

We children climbed rolling hills on our parent's ranch, usually barefoot when it warmed enough to take off our shoes. Ted and I ran on toughened feet all summer despite sharp sand burs. We brought in the milk cows from the pastures in the evenings, played in blowouts and ran through a water hose when the weather was hot. We roller skated, with clip on skates, round and round in our basement the only place we could skate. We played follow the leader on skates.

We went to town in Dad's old black Ford pickup, riding to Ainsworth with Dad and Jim when I had my first soda pop. It was extremely hot so Dad stopped in Johnstown when he bought a glass bottle of grape pop for five cents. The pop was hot and not the treat he expected. I got car sick riding in vehicles so I rarely did.

One morning our mother hurriedly made brownies for our school lunch. We looked forward to that lunch. The brownies smelled wonderfully appetizing—then we took a bite. They were awful!! Our mother forgot to add sugar. She felt really bad. I thought our hot lunches in high school were good.

Country Christmas programs were usually an evening event. We dressed up in clothes we had and felt we did good for school plays. We sang loud and every student memorized a recitation. Some teachers had never been in a rural school so they didn't show up - or teach. My first teacher reported shooting prairie dogs while riding her horse to school. She was teaching in March when I started school and the Goose Creek fire broke out. We girls spent the night on Floyd Keller's couch. I had just turned six and didn't know where my family was except for Jim. I was worried about our parents, baby and little brothers but kept quiet.

We learned to play tonettes and sang for our school programs. Patty, Mary Sue, Kay Lynn and I learned to tap dance for programs. Patty, Mary Sue and I did 'The Minuette', an old dance, with Jim, Ted and Tom. Our mothers made long dresses with ruffles in different colors. David was a good student and friend who often checked their button drawer to bring a button he thought might be different.

Box suppers were held to raise money for the school. We decorated boxes. An elderly man bought my first box. I didn't know him so Mom sat with me and ?. Patty and I made boxes for an Elsmere box social. We were 12 and enjoyed that more.

A cinch broke on Rusty's saddle at the school yard gate, Lila and I fell off. She landed on her arm breaking it—again! I landed on my head and it hurt. After that we walked to school or Daddy took us in bad weather in a wagon or in his rattly old black pickup.

Most of us graduated on the Cherry County 8th grade honor roll which surprised our parents. They thought we missed too many days with eight months of school for eight years and no kindergarten. There was no way to know when teachers came. Often we went to school and home again because the teacher didn't show up.

I began 9th grade with Lila and I staying with Uncle Albert, Aunt Inez, John and Ruth Ann Vasey to attend Alma High School. We knew only cousin John. Lila graduated where Mom did as a senior. I got an Alto saxophone. Mr. Vap asked me to play cymbals in the marching band. We played at games and in Kearney and Lincoln, marching through Lincoln and at a UN football game. This was the only university football game I ever saw. For class initiation, we freshmen wore gunny sacks; we looked like cave dwellers. Senior Don J tried to rub red lipstick on my nose. I was glad I was strong enough to hold him away. Picture day was the next day and I did not want a red nose!

The next year in Logan County High, I caught chicken pox and had an appendix attack. It hurt to walk up the steep stairs to classes after an appendectomy. Dad came for me at Mary Jane's house when I broke out with chicken pox. Her mother wrapped me in a quilt and started a fire to warm the room. I was most miserable itching day and night. One extremely cold night, when I stayed with Mary Jane, she set a small electric heater too close to the bed. We woke up to see red and orange flames dancing six to eight inches high on our bed covers, close to our noses. It was frightening! I joined Future Homemakers of America and attended State FHA convention in Kearney. And I was a candidate for State Vice President. Changing to Thomas County High ended that. We were closer to home and glad for that.

I caught the mumps as a junior, brothers Jim and Ted got them first. I sprained my ankle in a Physical Education soft ball game. The school nurse said my ankle could be broken so Mrs. Mercer drove me to a Valentine doctor. The next morning, we had a school fire drill. Superintendent scolded Eleanor and Carolyn for helping me limp outside. Jim, Ted and I went to basket ball games, class parties and church parties in Thedford. I was in several plays. The six seniors chose younger siblings for parts in their play so I was in Desperate Ambrose. One night during practice, I went upstairs to my room to get a prop at Florea's. I was shocked to find my roommate sharing my diary with her friends!

Trojan cheer leading with Eleanor, Carolyn and Rose was fun. We cheered wearing red corduroy dresses, our mothers made with a large "T" on the front. We did the Bunny Hop to a "T-R-O-J-A-N-S" cheer. I felt especially good to cheer with opposing cheerleaders at half times. I liked volleyball and played every year. I liked to spike and to serve.

I was Cherry County 4-H Queen in 1956, selected by judges on record books. Wanda called me, "Queen Elizabeth." I completed numerous 4-H projects, helped at Halsey 4-H camp and led a small 4-H club. I earned many 4-H medals. I convinced my children to try entomology, dog, cat, woodworking and a variety of 4-H projects too.

Senator Carl Curtis campaigned in Thedford when I was a junior. I saw him again at Fort Robinson while working as a hostess; I rang up his meal ticket 40 years later. He had aged! I probably had too. I met Congresswoman Virginia Smith when she spoke at Chadron State College. Andy, my four year old grandson, was with me. I took his picture with her holding his little hand. Country and Western singer, Hockshaw Hockins visited Chadron to sing one night. I got his autograph which was shortly before he was killed in a tragic airplane crash.

I was a junior when we got a telephone and electricity for the first time at home on the ranch. It was long distance, costing about $3, to call home so we didn't, except when Ted swelled with mumps and drove home alone. Jim and I thought our folks should know to watch for him.

Logan County High School English teacher, John Senator, was probably my best teacher. He was encouraging and positive. We were assigned to write a weekly essay and select the best writings for a booklet. My favorite teachers in college were Dr. Lyle Andrews. He gave credit for answers when it was not what he had in mind. He demonstrated experiments; Dr. Frank Thoendel who was a great teacher. I enjoyed his Industrial Art class and Dr. Doxtator, a Nebraska writing teacher. He was helpful to encourage teachers during a summer writing class.

Normal training required passing a test. I took Normal Training two years and did student teaching at the home school. That fall I taught five little students: Duane, Eddie, Mikel, Linda and Bonnie. They were so cute at the Cherry County Music Festival singing 'Red River Valley' dressed in white shirts with blue ribbon ties. I thought a lot of them and still do.

In grade school, I wore high top brown shoes, long cotton stockings and cotton dresses. High school clothes were skirts and blouses. Jeans were forbidden for girls! We wore turned down white anklets and cardigan sweaters over blouses. My college roommate, Jean, loaned me bright blouses after a teacher said I needed brighter clothes. Jean helped me pass teacher education training by offering her brilliant blouses.

My first train ride was from North Platte to Washington state. I was 19 and really thought Grandma Paine, at 80, was too old to travel alone. I made friends with an elderly lady who said her desire was to jump into piled fresh hay. She thought I was so fortunate to have done so. She didn't know stacking hay isn't 'fun.' I visited with a black lady about our teaching.

Little nephew called to me, "Bet". He said, "Bet, Hold my Lee." I spent time helping Lila with Lee and Tom. The Ahrens replaced a worn out mattress after I woke up with nightmares strangled in a sheet in a deep spring coil hole. I slept better without the holey mattress.

Television came to the Sandhills after I graduated from high school. We watched the Rose Parade at home in black and white the following year. My dad enjoyed Television country music naming all the performers on sight. My mother liked The Dinah Shore show.

Advice to others: resolve not to be afraid to do what is right and important. I determined to not do what I'd regret, trust in the Lord and pray about decisions. God has promised to be with you. Don't go where you would be ashamed to be seen by your family or by God. I deeply regret re-marriage. I have made mistakes and I am sorry. I ask my family for forgiveness.

Thirty years, after I graduated from CSC with a two year degree I earned my Bachelors degree. I took night classes and correspondence classes. The last semester was required on campus. There were deep drifts that January. Snow drifts and my little grandsons plus my children made fun pictures to develop for journalism and photography classes. I still take classes every five years to renew my teaching certificate to be eligible to qualify to substitute teach which I've done since 1962.

My Grandmas were 'most admired.' They laughed a lot, were fun, gracious and caring. Grandma Paine and Grandma Weber wrote letters and sent cards. Grandma Paine sewed and later hand pieced and stitched quilts. Our family had good times with our Grandmas.

Ted and I walked every isle in the Ainsworth dime store. I don't remember buying or having coins to buy with. We looked at many things we had never seen before. Dad gave Lila a $10 bill for class dues and needs in Alma for us. Dues were a dollar a semester. Lila spent the last of the money on blouses for each of us at the end of the school year.

Thanksgiving was at our Weber Grandparents home. A roasted hen or turkey was featured with others contributing. I remember an attractive tablecloth embroidered by our Mama as a gift covered the table. Grandma Weber fixed mashed potatoes and gravy, home raised beans, real cream and mincemeat pie. Our mother usually added chocolate cake, Jello and baked hot rolls. We sat on boards on ten gallon cans. if anyone moved they pinched! Great Grandmother offered prayer of thanks for God's blessing on the meal and the gathering. Women and girls did the dishes together.

Favorite movie stars were Elizabeth Taylor, Margaret O'Brien and June Allison. They were beautiful and seemed respectable. News media didn't reveal dirt - bad stories like they do today. Our family watched them in the movies Little Women and The Secret

Garden which we enjoyed. They were good actresses. We very rarely saw movies.

August 13, 1956, Mom, Dad, Glen, Gene and I were at the east section picking apples, when Jim came driving fast. He told us, "Ted was hurt in an accident and is in the Broken Bow Hospital." Our folks took off immediately across rough country trail roads to Broken Bow. Mom stayed with Ted for months until he was transferred to Omaha. She called home daily to report. Mrs. Hanna called to ask how Ted was and to offer encouragement. Ted was unconscious for three months. I spent many nights praying for him. I was in college when Mom wrote, "Ted is waking." Thats when I let the tears fall. Jim and I drove from Chadron to Broken Bow to see Ted and we weren't allowed in. Mom had gone home that day. She said she would have seen that we got in. Jim and I saw Ted on Thanksgiving, he had dropped from 180 to about 90 pounds. He walked with a rail Dad fixed in the living room to the bathroom. Nurse Josie helped with Ted's rehabilitation. The first thing Ted asked me was what cars he drove in high school. Doctors told our folks they didn't think Ted could survive. They gave him less than a 50% chance. I feel certain our Mom, Dad and many prayers helped.

Pay for teaching, in 1955-1956 was $250 a month. I saved it all for college. My first call from Harold came on March 30,1958, near the end of my second year of college. We saw a lot of movies that spring. He was kind, caring and interested in many things. We wrote the following year and he came to see me every month or two. One dark night we got lost looking for the snow trails to my boarding place. He proposed under a tree along the high way by Cody. We were married in the Chadron Baptist Church on May 24,1959 by Rev. Stanley Malmgren. Grandma Weber served the cake I had made and decorated for a small family wedding. Lila and Johnny stood up with us. Ted was in charge of the guest book.

I taught the Ormesher school south of Valentine after college. I taught kindergarten in Crawford in 1960. Two little kindergarten boys fell into the mud. I called their mothers to please bring dry britches. I had 42 different students in split sessions, with no aides. I missed one day of teaching school, when I went to the doctor for morning sickness. School Superintendent, Orin White, offered me a job for the following year. I stuttered, "I can't." I wanted to be a stay at home mother. Jerry arrived October 18, 1960. I never taught full time again but began substitute teaching.

Harold and I were outside finishing chores one dark night watching a strange light jump east of us near the buttes. My mother called right then to say her double cousin Nell Paine was found dead in Africa, where she worked. I referred to the bouncing bright light as an Unidentified Flying Object (UFO). We may never know but I believe it was.

Grandma Paine and Grandma Weber were widowed at 61 years. I was widowed at 55; we had a common legacy. My daughter Kristi was widowed and alone at 36. We didn't want to share this. Prayer and faith helps us survive tough times. We hopefully can encourage others. I tell married women, "I am so thankful told Harold I loved him every day. Don't put off telling others you love them." Only other widows can understand the loneliness and pain of being alone. Good friends develop through trials.

Beginning in 1992, I taught a variety of programs in schools all over through the Dawes County Extension School Enrichment programs directed by Shari Meyer. I took Patriotic Programs making flag pins with beads and safety pins to schools and International programs with students from all over to city and rural schools. I arranged students and International people to meet several times in Sioux and Dawes County for learning experiences. Students studied countries represented and high schoolers prepared recipes from other countries for an International meal. I did educational programs on coal, wheat, 1880s, TRAP (Tobacco Risk Awareness Program), Intergenerational, calligraphy, and old clothes on dolls. It was learning experiences. I took programs to youth groups when requested. I still do substitute teaching when called. There were many rural schools and the town schools called too.

Published writings began for me with short stories in Capper's Weekly. I wrote 'Imogene and the Traveling Trunk,' which won first place and $25 in a Dawes County Old Timer's Tales in 1968. A radio announcer condensed and read the story on the radio. I wrote "The Tindale-Vasey Voyage" from notes I took from Grandma and Mom about our ancestors in England in 1970-71. Mom and Elsie Paine shared information. I was down with a threatened pregnancy so I spent my time writing. I learned family history and made multiple copies to share with Vasey and Paine relatives. In 1993, I wrote "Alone", about working on the farm after Harold's death which is in <u>Leaning into The Wind.</u> I wrote **"When the Lights Came On"** which is in <u>Circle of Brightness</u>. An airline sent a T-shirt for writing about flying. My poems, "Sandhills Serenity" and "Grandchildren," are in a London book. A travel story I wrote won $100 in an International contest in 2004. My poems, "Why" and "Veterans" are in the American Legion Auxiliary magazine. A salad recipe is in a "Nebraska Life" book. My poem "Sandhills Sunshine," won $20, first place at state Family and Community Education (FCE) in 2010. My stories are published in Nebraska Farmer, Nebraskaland Rural Electric, Crawford Clipper, Chadron Record, Thomas County Herald, Rodeo News, Range Magazine and Dawes County Senior Currier. I have pictures on The Fence Post cover.

Time spent with grandchildren is my greatest joy. I am thrilled when they visit. or call. They, and their parents, are more important than anything except faith which sustains me. I have joy and hope for better days. I expect to see loved ones in Heaven. Alyssa often prays, "Thank you God for food and God bless my Daddy, Mommy, Grandma and Cody in Iraq."

Good memories are shared experiences: Cody and Ashley planting flowers in my yard for Mother's Day. Tiny Will and Joey running to me, each holding a fuzzy white kitty slipper. They felt so good to be surprising their Grandma. One time my father came out from the bedroom with a fuzzy slipper, grinning and announcing, "I found a cat under my bed!" A picture of our four grandsons by the barn door holding baby puppies is super special. I had that picture put on a sweat shirt which is 'our favorite.' My first store bought cake was for my college graduation from Kathy and Jerry, a lovely surprise. Thank You!

The year I drove a truck in a wheat field for Johnny Ahrens was my most frightening experience. I heard crackling noises and looked down seeing flames jumping through a hole under the truck shift in dry wheat stubble. I stopped and ran to flag down my brother in law, Johnny to help. My heart was pounding. Johnny responded, "Oh, Cats!" Marcus Cain watched from his tractor in a nearby field.

We didn't have Christmas trees because trees in the Sandhills were planted and not cut. Money was scarce so we didn't go to town or buy one. Lila bought a small plastic tree with gum drops for the table when she began teaching. After I married, we climbed high in the Gibbons hills looking for a perfect cedar tree, often on Harold's birthday. He looked forward to taking the family 'tree hunting.' He'd spot a tree, while checking his cattle, then return to locate it.

School programs included a nativity scene and Christmas songs. The prettiest Mary I ever saw was little brother when there were no girls in the country school. Alyssa was a beautiful Mary in 2007, holding her life like doll for a nativity scene at Open Door Church.

A favorite tradition just before our school programs was when our mother would say, "I think you should open this package early." My children really liked that idea. It would be an item of needed clothing. We loved the tradition. A pink sweater was one such gift. My best gifts were our babies and then our grand babies and great grand babies. They are gifts from God and so precious. At eight, Wayne said, "Our baby is the best Christmas Present." He put a bow on eight month Kristi for a picture. Jerry was two months and Wayne three for their first Christmas. Special times were showing them tree lights and watch their eyes sparkle.

My experiences with Santa were limited. 'He' came to school when I was in the 6th grade wearing <u>my</u> snow boots! I asked kindergärtner Bonnie's older brother Floyd to be Santa when I taught. She later told me, "I know who Santa is 'cause I saw Floyd's class ring." Jimmy D tried to run outside to check when Santa said his reindeer were on the school roof.

I prepared New Years meals for the Gibbons; it was their anniversary. She was a good cook and especially enjoyed time with their grandchildren. She was 68 when Jerry, their first grandchild was born. She died January 18, 1974 when Kristi was not quite three. Kristi got red boots for Christmas that year and thought they were from her Grandparents. Wayne was 11 and Jerry 13. They loved her and climbed outside a hospital window to see her. She excitedly waved. Gramps lived alone for ten years. He said he'd give up all his modern utilities before his telephone. Our family called him every day. That's when we learned how very important those calls were to him.

A favorite gift I gave to my parents was a red Rose Quilt I designed and sewed for their 40th anniversary. I put names and birthdays, of my parents, their parents and grandparents plus their children on the red roses. The grandchildren were represented by rosebuds. I made and decorated an anniversary cake for them which our family delivered. Kristi was little and I took her picture with Mom. I have that quilt. For their 50th Anniversary, I sent blocks to all the family members near and far. I requested they decorate the block with a shared memory for a quilt. My favorites were the governor's table with cat tracks, Blue—their three legged dog, a pheasant, a bee and a jar of honey, straw stacks. Some weren't ever returned. Lila bought quilted material and I sewed them on. Lila has that quilt. We gathered for cake on our folks 25th, 40th and 50th. Their 50th was late because Mom refused to celebrate until Jim was out of the hospital from his horse rollover accident. We met in the Halsey shelter and Aunt Florence helped decorate with yellow roses and streamers. Grandma Weber came from Lincoln. Dad bought her a wrist watch as their special guest honor. Many friends stopped by to sign their book and visit with the family. I gave them a book of 5X7 enlargements of special events in their lives.

We rode horses to school as did our neighbors. The older boys instigated a race which big brother could not refuse. I don't know who won but I know our parents were emphatic, "No more horse racing." Ted and I spent time playing with Rusty during summer months. If we slid off he would wait for us to brush off and climb on again. We laid on Rusty's back enjoying the summer sunshine. When he accidentally stepped on our bare feet, he'd carefully move his hoof. One time I rode Rusty across our water way when he decided to lay down and roll. I kicked his sides until he finally changed his mind and walked out. It wasn't deep but I didn't want rolled on in the water. Horseback riding is common in the country. I rode a lot. Does that make me a cowgirl? I have never owned a pair of boots or a cowboy hat.

COWBOY DADDY

Cowboys have rules for living; they give the other guy an advantage of any doubt. A cowboy's word and handshake are his honor. Cowboys work hard every day taking care of and protecting their family and livestock—a good dog, plus cows and horses, chickens and turkeys. The cowboys I know use short bits of wisdom. They talk briefly but make what is said count. My dad was a cowboy all his life. He broke horses to work in the hayfield, then used them to rope and ride on his ranch. He raised a large herd of cattle along with a big garden and a host of fine friends. He was kind and thoughtful. He forbid abuse of animals, language or friends.

Our cowboy Daddy rode his black horse for years. He used his horses for pulling on haystacks. He taught them to turn by calling 'gee' or 'haw.' He preferred Hereford cattle until advantages of crossbred cattle were proven in the Sandhills. He selected Angus and Hereford to raise the best cattle cross possible. Daddy demonstrated drinking from the creek and windmill 'cowboy style.' He made his own spurs, which I never saw him wear. Our folks discouraged riding for sport.

Our mother was the love of Dad's life. She was a stay at home mom who could ride, mow hay or milk cows. Daddy took us along on the hay sled to feed cattle on cold winter days. Standards of cowboy country living are changing. This makes reminiscing and sharing all the more worthwhile. I hope to share love, faith and family values to my children, grandchildren and great grandchildren. Our parents taught us by living life doing what is right with a clear conscience. Our parents showed they cared by their actions and high expectations.

FROM MY MOTHER'S BIBLE

Blessed are they who understand
my faltering step and palsied hand.
Blessed are they who know that my ears today
must strain to catch the things they say.
Blessed are they who seem to know that
my eyes are dim and my wits are slow.
Blessed are they who looked away
when coffee spilled at the table today.
Blessed are they with a cherry smile
who stop to chat for a little while.
Blessed are they who never say,
'You've told that story twice today.'

Author unknown

The six of us: Jim, Glen, Lila in back with Beth, Gene and Ted in front, dressed for Easter in 1944.

NEW BEGINNINGS

I started school because Jim refused go alone. Lila was in the hospital with a broken arm. Donald Luther had rode his horse galloping into our yard to announce Lila was hurt. Dad hurried to get her and bring her home with a splint he had fixed. Mama tried to feed her but she refused food. Lila said, "Dad carried me and I was embarrassed because I was eight and he hadn't carried me for years." Dad stopped at Floyd Keller's for a driver so he could hold her on the bumpy trail road to Ainsworth. The next day her arm swelled and doctors wanted to amputate. They needed parental permission and Dad was fighting fire. Lila still has her arm though bent and scarred from stitches. I remember asking if she could use her hand and she jerked hard on my braid.

Granddaddy was a short little man with a cookie duster mustache and a jolly disposition. Jim and I visited our grandparents in Arnold when we attended Gandy,1952-`53. I am thankful we spent what time we could with them. I was sitting under the wall phone eating supper with the family when a call came to tell Dad that his father had passed on.

Grandma Paine liked for us to stay with her. She sewed jumpers for Lila and for me. I took a bath in her round galvanized wash tub then moved stepping back feeling clean and wearing clean clothes. I stepped back to get out of her way mopping and toppled over into the dirty water. I was terribly embarrassed. Grandma laughed and laughed.

We played often with our twin aunts, Flora and Florence, five years older than me. I was in 8th grade when Flora taught a rural school north of Valentine. She came home on weekends and hurried to ask what I did in school that week. She was teaching Elsie, a student near my grade. Florence was by then married to Alvin Joy.

Grandma Paine gave me her watch, my first, when I came home after my appendectomy in Arnold. I gave it to Cousin Judy after Harold gave me a watch for Christmas. I wonder what Judy did with Grandma's watch? Uncle Chester bought a $5 bicycle 'for the boys.' I am sure I rode it as much or more than they did. Gene was little but he learned to ride that bicycle by sliding his legs way over from side to side. We rode lots of miles on that blue bicycle in the sand.

Aunt Mildred stayed with us to teach our school when Lila was in first grade. I remember the family sitting around the supper table hearing coyotes howl. Three year old, Glen spoke up saying, "Maybe it's a rabbit!" I told Aunt Mildred, I knew Evening in Paris was her favorite perfume. She said, "Yes, and I spanked you for getting into it, I always regretted that." I told her she is forgiven. I was six and rearranged bottles and lipsticks on her dressing table. I played dolls always carried Bonnie Bell. Bonnie Bell is in front of my face in most pictures. I was given Marietta doll when I was 10. I made clothes of flour sacks but was old to play dolls.

Our parents punished us when they felt the need by using their hand or a razor strap. We were scolded and/or whipped. When I went inside a small building where Dad was auguring ground corn, I got a hard spanking. He said, "Grain dust is dangerous!"

Ted and I gathered eggs but we didn't like pecking setting hens. We decided to break a mean speckled hen by hanging her up by her foot. We forgot and found her too late. No one told us Jim claimed her and planned to hatch eggs. We children chattered up stairs in bed and folks scolded. Upstairs was one big room with a stairway and chimney in the middle.

We had a kitchen hand pump for water with a bucket under the drain to catch water. Scraps were carried outside to the pigs or chickens. Cooking was done on a wood burning range which heated the house. She ironed our clothes by heating flat irons on that old wood burning stove even in the summer time. Eventually, Mom got a kerosene stove which she liked, especially in the summer. She mopped floors daily to cool the rooms when it was hot. We had a large living room and dining room with two small bedrooms downstairs. Up stairs beds were in all four corners and one near the stairway chimney. I recall reciting Bible verses from a calendar each night. My clothes were remakes from Mildred's, the twins or Lila's stored in five or 10 gallon cans with mothballs. A favorite blue taffeta dress arrived in a box of outgrown clothes from Elsie's young neighbor. This box was special as the clothes fit only me.

GOING ON

Harold, Jerry, Wayne, Kristi and I helped rake leaves in Grandma and Gramps Gibbons yard. He joined raking while explaining, "Mold sticks to old leaves and makes us sick." He was wise. He grew a good garden, strawberries and the prettiest flowers.

Grandma Gibbons was a perfect housekeeper and very much loved their three grandchildren. She made sure she carried candy corn in her apron pockets for the little ones whenever they came driving in, which was often. They ran to her to reach into her apron pockets, which thrilled her. She liked to cook for holidays and get out her best dishes and silverware to set an impressive table. She used her tiny salt holders and linen table cloth on the table.

Gramps and Grandma kept napkins in a little drawer of their white kitchen drop leaf table. Jerry and Wayne stopped to see him after school. He looked forward to their visits.

I took a picture of Gramps with his roses on my Polaroid camera shortly before he died. He looked at the colored picture in amazement, wide eyed he asked, "What will they think of next?" He was 94 and still active in his yard. We respected and loved him. His knees ached so he would report when a storm was coming. We took turns sitting with him when he went to the hospital a few hours before he died, the only time I saw him in the hospital.

REMEMBERING

My grandmothers, parents and siblings were my biggest influence. I looked up to my aunts and my sister. They had high standards and strong faith. John F. Kennedy was assassinated while I was at home cooking with our two small sons at my feet. Grandma Gibbons called from Chadron telling me, "Turn on the radio." Harold had taken her to shop for shoes. She didn't get shoes but my nephew Nick was born that day. Both Grandmas laughed a lot. They lived to be 99 and almost 97 years old. Recently I have read that to live to be old, laughter and a strong faith are necessary.

I began collecting buttons when Lila broke her arm. I sewed thousands of buttons on salt sacks my mother had hemmed for pages, 50 buttons to a page. Students brought buttons to school. Family members brought buttons from where ever they visited. The twins brought some neat ones for me from Uncle Fred and Aunt Ada Weber's button jar. I checked buttons at 4-H meetings and at the neighbors when they brought them out. My mother bought a few unusual new buttons. A button collecting pen pal and I exchanged buttons.

My first permanent was by students learning in Ainsworth. The electric heated things kept over heating so the girl blew on them to keep my head from burning. She repeatedly asked, "Where is it hot?"

Our family was sitting at the table eating breakfast when Daddy said, "Listen! Quiet!" The radio announced the bombing of Pearl Harbor. Fifty years later, I saw Pearl Harbor with bubbles still rising in the water around The Arizona. It was a sobering experience. I heard the radio tell of a neighbor's death from a fox hole fighting overseas. I didn't like to listen to the radio which operated on 32 volt batteries of electricity. We turned the radio on only during news and the news was not good.

GROWING UP COUNTRY

Growing up in the country with a house filled with brothers and a sister, we learned to make do and to entertain ourselves. We didn't have close neighbors. We spent time working and playing with each other. We helped our parents with outside chores plus cooking, learning to make pancakes, bread and cakes. My brothers wanted to clean out the bowl after I made chocolate cakes. I told them to make their own cakes. Then I helped them learn to make and bake cakes. Mixes weren't invented yet.

I remember drawing pictures, cutting, coloring in color books or on plain paper and writing letters to our family. We had fun making May Day baskets with wild flowers for our teachers. Dad showed me how to cut out paper dolls when I was little. I was pleased with them. Years later I showed my children, nieces and others how to cut paper dolls from paper the way Dad taught me. We made Valentines from wallpaper sample books and seed catalog pictures. We tried crepe paper flowers, coloring and reading. Mama read books on stormy days or in the evenings like Beautiful Joe, Bambi and Old Yeller.

We children stayed outside when it was nice, helping with chores or walking around the grass covered hills. The dog and cats were company wherever we went.

No one ever said, "I'm bored." We found things to do or our mother would find work in the garden or house for us. There were weeds to pull, insects to catch and balls to throw. We climbed trees moving from tree top to tree top. We made dirt playhouses under the trees. I followed Daddy as he plowed deep furrows between trees. I held the reins pretending I was farming.

My sister whipped great looking mud pies. I preferred to rock my dolls. I always wanted a doll I could bathe. I never did have one. Our family had animals—dog, horses, cats, chickens and pigs. We were excited when we found new baby kittens or puppies. Daddy took us to the barn to see baby pigs or calves. I often played with kittens and looked for eggs.

Little brother Gene climbed the ladder in the barn with Jim, Ted and I. He pulled a rope stepping backwards in the hay mow. He dropped through a hole for feeding cattle and/or horses. Brothers and I rushed down to get him. The wind was knocked out of him and we were terribly scared. I carefully carried him to the house while worried brothers followed close.

Ila Jean Hanson from New York, whose mother Ruby was a college friend of our Mothers,' came to visit. She rode horses and told about falling on cactus. She came to our house and made a floral wreath for "Queen for a day." Lila was the oldest so we made wild violets woven into a crown for her hair and a bouquet for her. I remember Ila Jean making clever Valentines for us every year that we greatly enjoyed.

Ted and I climbed on Rusty by sliding up his neck as he grazed and raised his head. We slid down his neck and turned around to ride. I have never been ashamed of growing up in the country. Some people said, "They are hicks from the sticks." If hicks means country living, I am thankful my family had the benefit of growing up in the country far from noises and fumigation of city life. We were happy in the country. We didn't know the benefits of telephone, electricity, paved roads or close neighbors.

EARLY DAYS

I arrived in my parents' home in March with no doctor. Lila said Great Grandmother Giles rocked her and Jim to sleep. She was almost three and he was 18 months. She said, "You were a red wrinkled baby." I thought of myself as ugly. I weighed six pounds on the kitchen scale but Mama said she didn't think I weighed that much. She said I had rickets, causing bowed legs. We were required to wear shorts for college gym class so finally I adapted and began to forget about my bowed legs.

Grandma Etta and Great Great Grandmother Elizabeth attended my birth. My mother said she was hanging wallpaper when her water broke, two weeks early. She had asked her doctor for calcium as she knew she and I needed it. Doctor said he'd give vitamins and calcium after I arrived. My parents named me Elizabeth Pauline.

An early memory was playing under a heavy square block quilt in a frame with brother Ted while our Mother tied quilts. We 'helped' by pushing the needle up through the material. A quilt frame was up on January 29,1940, when Glen was born at home. I was standing on a chair beside the round breakfast table when a man wearing a black coat and hat hurried in. I later learned it was the doctor. White frost designs covered the cold windows. Lila said the doctor took her to school in his fine car that morning.

Baby pictures of me alone are extremely rare. I watched Mama wrap a quarter with film to mail in for three cents postage for developing. This was depression years and our folks were poor though we children didn't know it. Mom always managed to get groups in pictures.

Home was a yellow frame house north of Elsmere—population three. Roads were trails made by pickup tracks in sand through the rolling hills. Franklin D. Roosevelt was president. We heard him on our 32 volt battery radio reassuring people during WWII. One afternoon we walked home from school, finding our mother in tears. She reported, "The president died."

I helped Mama embroidery lazy daisies on tiny flannel blankets and gowns for 'our new baby.' Grandma held me up and asked if I knew which was 'our baby' in the hospital. I knew for I saw the flannel blankets I had helped my mother make. Grandma was surprised that I knew Baby Gene.

Our Mama was born, February 13, 1909 in her parents' home near Oxford, Nebraska to Claude Seth and Henrietta Ellen (Etta) Vasey Paine who married on March 16, 1907 the day before her 26th birthday. The Paine family came from Illinois, a few weeks before Grandpa's birth. Their sod home was flooded and Great Grandma Minerva (Covell) Paine scooped out water. Great Grandpa Cassius, Charlie, Mertie, and Maud paddled in a row boat and climbed through the window. The Covell ancestors came from Illinois. Sgt. Marcellus J Covell and Melissa Covell were both in the Civil War.

Grandma Paine told me our mother didn't have a name for ten days. She said, "I think Irene is the prettiest name." I agreed. We named our baby Kristi Irene for her Grandma and Great Grandma. Mom's family moved to a place owned by Uncle Fulwar Paine and his wife Ellen, a teacher. They had William, George and Lois. Mom, Dad, Gene, Harold, Kristi and I met George in Portland in 1985. He was a delightful gentleman who loved to talk. He raised beautiful pansies which he dried and included in every letter. His driving was hair raising in Portland. He was a special guy who was thrilled to show us the sights. We had a good time with him. He told about his glass eye and other family stories. George Franklin was named for his uncle by the same name, shot in the Civil War. George adopted Norman who had John, Jeff and Jennifer. George told me, "I was not going to continue bad teeth in the family."

Mom was seven with long dark braids when she began school in District 102. She said she wrapped her braids around her ears to keep warm while riding her horse Sleepy to school. She grew up and taught the home school. She told us the little Jelinek boys, whose parents sold the place to our folks, got dolls from relatives and buried them. I always wondered where they were buried. Eventually, I decided they most likely were cloth and had rotted.

Ted and I at two and three sitting by a tree, about when he said he was going to grow a beard and smoke a pipe.

TED AND ME

Standing in our corral by the red barn one bright sun shinny day, cheerful, black eyed Ted announced he was going to grow up, smoke a pipe and grow a black beard. I was four and terribly upset at the thought of my best friend, cherubic three year old brother, wearing a black beard and smoking a smelly pipe. I was disturbed at such a revolting idea.

Ted bent over with laughter, giggling. I was so upset I told him, "No you won't, I won't let you!" We stood there with me crying and Ted laughing. Older brother and sister thought it was funny. Ted still giggles about that exchange when it is mentioned.

Some days Ted and I walked around our section finding insets, grasshoppers and butterflies in our path. We made up and played games. It was fun doing things together. Our job was to gather eggs and we faithfully did our job protesting the pecking setting hens.

Ted and Jim gave our dolls rides on their stick horses when we played under the Box Elder trees. We used branches to 'sweep' the play area. Daddy cut our brothers' hair. We discovered each country boy had hair cuts styled by their fathers. Our parents did not ever demonstrate affection with hugs or kisses. They were involved in our activities and ready to answer questions. They organized a 4-H club and a Sunday School, which met in our school.

Dad drove Ted and me to Maranatha Bible Camp near North Platte and to Camp Witness by Long Pine. Some people called us 'missionary girls' when I was teaching Bible school with Esther. My mother called when I taught north of Mullen to say Great Grandmother Giles had died. Elsmere was a church Grandmother had organized so I taught Bible School at Elsmere the following week as I had promised. I missed her funeral but I know she would have approved.

One dark night we were playing crack the whip with the neighbor kids at Voss' house after a 4-H meeting. I was on the end running fast when I fell. I hollered and was lifted into their little wagon and pulled to the kitchen where their mother, Marjorie pulled a big long rusty nail out of my knee. The next day Jerry rode his horse over to ask how my knee was. It hurt and was swollen big. Several days later Dad asked if I wanted to see a doctor. I said, "No." That afternoon mom and I squeezed out lots of thick yellow puss. Finally, my knee began to heal.

Tippy was our grandparents' shaggy black and white dog. He chased Granddaddy's large white prancing saddle horse, Shorty. Tippy chased Shorty and kept his tail trimmed. Ted and Glen thought it was funny to watch Tippy chase that horse. Tippy got kicked, Glen laughed, "One time I thought he was dead but he got up again." The horse was called Shorty because of his shortened white tail. Tippy ignored all the other horses.

Ted and I double dated with friends in high school. He enjoyed many girlfriends and driving around Thedford. He and I maintained a close bond.

The country was always home. Our parents were tireless workers and they planted thousands of little evergreen and deciduous trees. Dad hand planted windbreaks and shelter belts of various trees. He liked fruit trees and enjoyed harvesting apples and crab apples. He knew each variety and told us which was which. We were harvesting apples when Jim came driving fast to tell us, "Ted is in Broken Bow Hospital"—a car accident.

Ted and I had never seen a black person when he asked how we would feel if we did. His hospital roommate in Omaha was a lonesome black man paralyzed from a gun shot in his spine. Ted asked me to write to this new friend. I did and received several appreciative notes. Ted came home at Thanksgiving. He was thin and shaky. It was hard to readjust. He asked many questions about his past trying to reestablish the months he had been unconscious. We now have good friends from all over the world.

FEED SACKS

Our family chose chicken feed and flour by the print on the sacks they were in. There were huge piles of sacks, according to a small girl's memory. My mother made a dress for me of yellow honey bee print material. It was pretty and I used scraps to make a dress for Marietta, my doll. I wore that dress in a group picture taken with Great Grandmother. Another dress was a pink print. Some seemed wild but I chose subdued printed sacks.

Sacks were sewed into shirts for younger brothers. They wore them happily as we didn't have a choice. New sack clothes that covered us comfortably were fine. We didn't worry about style. We enjoyed the soft cotton material. Our parents often came home bringing surprise printed feed sacks they chose and that was acceptable too. We were glad for their judgment.

Once a seed company put together a style show of clothes made from sacks. I was the only skinny kid that a skimpy little sun-dress fit. It had bare shoulders with straps. I was not comfortable wearing that outfit. A neighbor laughingly commented to my mother and I that he could sense by the look on my face I was uneasy wearing the bright sun-dress. Others I wore and modeled with pleasure but they didn't make the lasting impression the skimpy sun dress did.

Sacks made useful sheets and pillow cases too. It took four big, usually white, sacks for one sheet. I saw one not long ago among our parents' possessions. They were good sheets and worked fine. Gene's baby diapers were white flour sacks bleached and hemmed. Great Aunt Cora grabbed a flour sack diaper to wipe dishes at our house the afternoon after Grandpa's funeral. That incident provided laughter before all the dishes were rewashed, scalded and wiped again with clean sack dishtowels. I have fond memories of feed sacks used for dishtowels, baby diapers, my button book pages, straining milk into the separator and for our bed sheets.

String from the cloth sacks was wrapped into a large ball for a multitude of uses. This was a good project to get little ones involved while the family worked. Our parents' ingenuity impressed me then and it impresses me even more now when I realize how they managed with what they had and made a good life for all of us. Our mother was full of adages like, "Waste not want not" which are still true. We lived by adages as we made use of what we had, like using every scrap of material, feed sacks and string.

SPECIAL CHRISTMAS

Snowflakes skittered across the evening sky. Frost wove intricate patterns over the cold windows. Five small children watched through scratched peep holes in the frost covered windows for sight of Dad's vehicle lights winding down the narrow tree lined driveway. Our baby brother slept peacefully in his crib.

A serious dark eyed innocent five year old waited anticipating the arrival of father home from an infrequent trip to town over rough country miles. The children stood ready to help unpack cardboard boxes of groceries to the shelves. Big boxes were to play in.

Smells of supper fragmented the room as a busy mother prepared food over a warm wood burning kitchen cook stove for a simple evening meal. The two little girls set the silverware on the table while their mother stalled the hungry children saying, "Take a drink of water." And, "Daddy will be home soon."

The sound of the old Ford pickup was heard with lights flickering as it rattled down the lane. Wide-eyed children stood as silent guards when snow covered father, smiling white haired grandmother in her long dark coat and aunt carried in boxes and packages.

Groceries were quickly put away in cupboards with help of many little hands. There was a case containing round boxes of oatmeal. Supper was bowls of steaming potato and beef soup and warm home made chocolate pudding. The table was soon cleared, as dishes were washed, dried and put away.

The family quickly gravitated to the living room near the warm wood burning heater. They stood wondering around a big round table piled with packages. Jolly adults began handing out packages. There were gifts for everyone!

This was 1942; packages were wrapped in heavy brown paper and tied with white string. We didn't know or care that in far distant cities other people had bright colored wrappings and ribbons around their gifts. We were elated to be together as family in this warm comfortable room. There was a surprise for each one.

Younger brother Ted received a blue riding toy truck. A seemingly large oval box was handed to me. I carefully unwrapped the brown paper and walked over with the box handing it to my sister, Lila, three years older than I. She had wished for a doll, hadn't she? I felt sure this was her gift. She pushed the box back at me and began unwrapping her own oval shaped package. She found a lovely doll with eyes that really opened and shut!

Dark brown eyes opened wide as I, a five year old, realized this doll was for me. A doll of my own! I named her Bonnie Bell and carried her with me everywhere. Other activities of the evening went unnoticed. I busied myself with the thrill of owning my very own doll. Pictures for years showed me holding Bonnie Bell doll close in front of my face. I was interested only in my doll.

Every year, I think back to that long ago Christmas and the thrill of owning my very own doll. I will always be grateful to my parents for the gift that made a quiet little girl feel special. This was truly a Christmas to remember.

GOOSECREEK FIRE

On March 3, 1943, a fire started by unknown sources. Some said a hired man lit a cigarette while opening a gate. One said it was vehicle friction or an electric fence spark by the gate. Fire was soon blazing hot, flamed by strong winds which continuing all day. Estimates say it burned a strip 35 miles long and three miles wide. Volunteer firefighters came from miles. No lives were lost but a barn and several outbuildings were destroyed. Nearly a thousand big hay stacks, 5000 tons, of good meadow hay burned. Hogs, horses and a calf were burned. Our Dad took his tractor and plowed a fire guard around our section of land and along the road to our place. Signs of plowed ground are still visible 50 years later.

The day before Lila had fallen off Luther's horse and broke her arm. She was in the hospital so I began attending school. Dad was plowing a fire guard around our place to stop the fire from spreading.

Grandpa Paine wrote to his sisters, "Lila fell off a horse playing after school Tuesday. Paul took her to Ainsworth that night then started up here to his folks on the 3rd. He saw the smoke on the way up. Irene and kids stayed here. I went with him. He went on west with a bunch backfiring. I went east as it had started up behind a bunch down on the meadow. I was told there was telephone call for him from the hospital but I did not see him again. Bessie Smith, (only people with a phone) went to Larsen's where Quinton was picking corn. They went to Paul's then the school house where Jimmie told them his folks had gone to Weber's. So they went up there then back here.

"Irene and Etta took our car and went for Ainsworth. They left a note on the table here and one at his place. He did not stop here nor go into the house when he got home but took the tractor and went to plowing until the fire was out. They stayed in town and he went up the next day. Lila's arm was broke near elbow and another bone slipped joint. The setting had slipped and her arm swelled. It had stopped circulation and they thought they might have to operate and according to law must have parents written consent."

Grandpa enclosed a clipping with a headline, "'Blaze destroys 5,000 tons hay. There was more than 1000 ranchers and residents of the area fighting the blaze,—the worst prairie fire in the history of this Sandhills area."

Our mother did not sign a release to amputate Lila's arm. Dad was fighting fire and couldn't be located. I recalled some of this and gleaned more from Grandpa's letter to his sisters. We students were driven to the Key's place where we waited all day. People sat and talked. I didn't know anyone; there was a baby but it wasn't 'our baby.' I wondered where my folks were and was a concerned. This was my first day of school!

That night we were driven back to Floyd Keller's. I remember horrible smells and the sight of bright haystacks blazing and sparking scattered in a wide area along Goose Creek Meadow as we traveled. A thought that remained with me was, "This must be what hell looks like."

MEMORIES LIVE ON

Roaming Nebraska's Sandhills I sense sharp images of long ago. Pause and listen as the past comes alive with sounds and visions of yesteryear. Let your imagination run free through these green sandy grass covered hills. Listen to a trill of a meadow lark or the caw of a flock of crows flying over a rustling grove of trees. Coyotes howl in the distant hills at sunset. Bright sun is sinking behind the hills then the thunder roars; clouds blow and churn on the horizon; lightening illuminates brilliant designs over the prairie.

Horses hooves pound across grassy plains running hard. Ox hoofs plunking with a wooden wagon rattling behind on a trail bringing an unknown visitor in early days to visit an isolated sod house family. Visitors walk across pine wood floor inside a soddie noticing the Elizabeth Post Office operating in a roll top desk in that warm cozy home; fragrances of food cooking fill our senses. Grandma contentedly stirs pudding and checks on her hot biscuits. The screen door squeaks as neighbors stop in to see if they have letters in the mail.

An old vehicle is driven slowly over long winding rough trails to a distant town when our youthful daddy broke his collar bone. He sits in the back with his kindly grandfather. Listen to the irregular sound of that old black Model T motor on rough spots; he doesn't complain. Sand flies as the car bumps nosily down the wheel trail path leaving sand tracks—until a gentle breeze sweeps them away. A smoky exhaust billows behind them.

Hear cows bawling loudly? They are rounded up and separated from their weaning calves. Calves are herded by young cowboys and their dad on horses to a loading chute. A years worth of work waits in that single paycheck.

Listen for laughter as an older cowboy, spurs jingling, mounts his horse and trots into the bright sunset toward home. Squeaking saddle leather is heard as the rider lopes easily along the hills. He dismounts quietly beside his barn door and gives his clothes a good shake before going inside. He takes off the saddle and bridle, sets out a bucket of oats and opens a gate before thinking of his own hunger. A smile crosses his face as he gives his trusty four legged friend a pat and bush down. A warm supper awaits on the iron range cook stove inside his dimly lit home along with a pleasant smiling wife and cheerful children running towards him greeting him with questions.

In the bright sunshine Daddy stitches an injured calf with his large curved needle and heavy brown thread pulling it through tough hide with his handy pliers. The calf recovers. The same pliers he carries everywhere in a pocket and uses to put rings in the sows noses and pull cactus from his hurting cattle or porcupine needles from his dog.

Daddy sits on squeaky porch step speaking softly to his family at the end of another day. Hear the clopping beat of horses trotting feet heading heading home. Cowboys air dry their clothes from a rare shower, noticing with appreciation a brilliant rainbow arching across an eastern sky. Windmill squeaks as it's wheel turns caught by a sudden breeze.

On a hot summer morning in the hayfield Granddaddy tosses his pitchfork off the top of a new hay stack. Dad catches the fork in the palm of his hand where it hangs momentarily until he quickly grabs the handle with his left hand. Dad warned us never to toss a pitch fork before looking below. We remember. The vision of his quick action remains.

Grandma's sparkling gray eyes remind us of her love of family after birthing ten children at home, seven survive. She cooks an abundant supply of tasty home grown beef, vegetables and fruit. She hoes the garden for relaxation and to keep a food supply growing. She bows her head and clasps her aging hands in quiet prayer as she closes her eyes and talks to the Lord. She prays expressing thankfulness for gifts of a warm home, food, a loving family with delight in many grandchildren and for strength to survive daily hardships. She smiles when she sees sons and daughters come to visit. Grandchildren bring laugh lines to her face and a bright sparkle in her eyes. She quickly begins cooking again.

A smelly old 'privie' door bangs in the wind on a path out back. It's a well worn trail we quickly run, especially in cold weather. Cold wind whistles while we wait. Old catalogs rustle in the breezes as a useful paper supply.

Dad speaks quietly to Red Satin, a soft young colt as he offers a bite of grain from a small dented tin bucket, rubs her ears and stretches a rope halter over her head. Quiet and good natured, Satin follows her benefactors, even up the stairs into their home. She goes out again stepping easily down the steps.

Hear the animals grunt as father encourages his four-horse team to pull a load of hay beside an isolated country school. He calls to urge black shiny Kate and gray Nell to pull harder as they strain to move an extra large haystack. Children sitting quietly in their desks listen and watch the action as a rare reprieve from studies. Books might be interesting but live action is more memorable at the moment.

Brothers pull kicking calves to our dad beside a hot smoky branding fire. I pull my cotton skirt over my nose to lessen the smoke as I hurry to carry a refilled vaccination needle to cowboy brother branders and Dad. I turn to look away when my Dad got out his knife to castrate and then de-horn bawling baby calves. We are content to be helping as part of 'the crew.' We come inside to clean up before for lunch smelling of burn seared calf hide and smoky fire. If there is a big herd we finish after eating.

Our parents peer intently through cold frost covered windows watching the fast falling snow. They watch and wait as we walk home from school. We ride horses some when snow is too deep or too cold for the pickup to start. Heavy snow pants protect but I'm still not warm. Horses run to the barn and begin eating before we head to the house for a hot supper waiting on the wood stove. Family eats healthy beef stew while seated around the big round table. Snow squeaks and crunches under foot as we tromp through deep drifts and make snow angels. Snow sparkles like diamonds glittering before our eyes.

Jeff, our much loved black and white fuzzy dog, waits in the driveway for his turn of recognition and appreciation for his watchfulness. "Good dog!" he hears from the children. He gets hugs and loving head pats from each youngster as he loudly thumps his bushy tail. On warm days children walk shuffling in loose sand to school and back in the trail road. We join neighbors for a short walk before branching towards home after school.

On windy days we searched for tumble weeds to speed our steps along the trail home. It was a challenge to be first inside where our mother and fresh oven scents of home made bread were waiting.

Hearing the mews of new baby kittens hiding in the haymow brings a special joy. We take turns choosing a favorite fuzzy baby and spend hours with our kitten. Calves are treated responsibly. They provide income for country living.

Chilled baby calves are brought inside near the wood fueled heating stove. All hands are activated to rub rags vigorously to restart circulation in animals' cold ears, legs and feet. We cheer as a calf begins to stand on wobbly legs and suck our fingers. Baby chickens, turkeys and ducklings are a challenge. Daddy brings in a squealing baby pig for the family to warm by the stove, feed, admire and touch.

Ted and I chase grasshoppers as we chatter for two and a half miles to school. We arrive in time to share lunch outside with the students before Daddy comes driving into the school yard after us in his rattly black Ford pickup. Years later, I see where teacher wrote 'Beth, Teddy and Jeff' as visitors. Our parents said, "Pretty soon," when I asked if it was time to meet Lila and Jim walking home from school so we began slowly. We planned to give the grasshoppers to our chickens and turkeys.

Bed time comes early on dark winter days. We listen to Mama read books by the evening light of a bare light bulb we settle in beds contentedly. Her voice continues until we get sleepy. Winds continue to move sifting sands. We are content to be considered children of the Sandhills.

TOGETHERNESS

Our family learned skills involved helping our parents on the ranch. We didn't consider not helping. I began driving the stacker tractor and rake before graduating to stacking hay with a pitchfork on top of a wire cage stacker with prairie hay or sometimes alfalfa or sweet clover. We didn't have rattle snakes so a rare snake was not the fright factor that is would be in Western Nebraska. Each of us had a job and fulfilled our part to the best we could. Helping with work was expected and we responded learning as we worked beside our parents.

A family outing most often to get the family members together in an activity. Activities may include climbing a hill or going for a sleigh ride. My mother was good at improvising to make us feel we were needed and involved. It was often chores or sharing with our siblings.

We found places we liked and shared. Look at the smiles when we climbed into the new straw stack. It was a scratchy experience but we had loads of fun just sharing the time together.

Our sons were anxious to help their Daddy drive a tractor and to ride horses to roundup the cattle. The whole family was involved when branding time came. Little ones held the end of a rope to be a safe distance from kicking calves. That's what country living is. Everyone works on a farm or ranch. We learn skills and are needed. I remember once when our little daughter was thrilled to go with her Daddy to fish in a local creek. A picture of her fishing is one of my favorites because of the contented look on her face and closeness to her Daddy. He was watching and helping her bait the hook to throw out a line. They were best friends and she respected him. Days together away from the daily work on farm routine were very rare so she relished doing what they enjoyed. We took along a snack to share while on fishing trips and when we climbed Crow Butte one afternoon. Little one wore her boots too.

Grandchildren are the delight of any grandparent so we tried to spend time doing what ever they have going for the day. I have driven many miles to spend time watching my grandchildren in dances, track meets and sports. A hug of appreciation makes a wonderful satisfying memory. Taking pictures to record the event helps me remember.

I am thankful I took pictures of grandson Will's football game several weeks before he was badly injured in a car accident. We have happy memories to share. He still talks about the plays and players of his favorite game. His little brother Joey liked to watch and cheer. We were proud to have him there until cancer took him, way too young. We have happy memories. Fathers and mothers appreciate a lift with work or time with family and friends. Togetherness as a family is a goal worth working toward.

LOOKING BACK

Thinking about growing up in the country is a reminder of good times. Wild grasses growing and flowers peek through the sandy soil. I was impressed with wild violets and daisies. My siblings and I ran through tall grass to the garden where our parents planted rows of food producing seeds. They once planted peanuts in their garden. Sweet potatoes grew on another year. Wind howled and blizzards blew snow and sleet over the hills. The wind whistled around the windows as we scratched through decorative frost and ice to peek out through the cold frosty designs covering our window panes.

I listened to the radio programs my mother turned on each morning. One Saturday the Susie and Johnny Brumfield stories touched my heart. I went around the corner knelt on my knees and prayed for Jesus to forgive my sins and take over my life. He was with me from then on. I had peace and was pressing to do what I had talents for and what was right.

One warm spring day, a soft breeze ruffled the grasses, as we helped construct a sod chicken house. Our Dad had plowed the deep furrows of though sod. We handed heavy clods of sod to Daddy to position into walls. We felt good 'helping' build that sod structure. We helped Daddy plant trees and work in the garden, which was essential for food. We were only around our family those early years. Mail carrier stopped to help sister try on her first pair of glasses. She showed Lila how much better she could see. "The teacher read the stories to me because I couldn't see the words," Lila later confessed.

We started in 4-H and worked diligently on a variety of projects. The county fair was 50 miles away so we didn't take animals after brothers had calves that first year. I took sewing and cooking projects and looked forward to the competition and making new friends. I felt honored when a mother asked me to show a calf for her daughter who had suffered a heat stroke.

College and teaching were included in my goals. I looked in a big scholarship book and asked the superintendent. He laughed,

"Scholarships are only for the top students," he scoffed. My most important teaching is my children and grandchildren! Education is helpful at home and school.

CHRISTMAS

Christmas years ago was celebrated as a time to pay tribute to our Lord and his gift to us. We gathered with family to share a meal around the large round wooden table. Our Great Grandmother Giles asked God's blessing. We didn't have evergreen trees in the Sandhills—unless we planted them. No one cut trees down!

Sister called to ask if I remembered early Christmas celebrations. There were no flash cameras so we have no pictures. Gifts were clothes needed. A new sweater or socks were cherished. We discussed Christmases past—brainstormed our memories. One year we hung stockings. Our long tan cotton stockings, worn in wintertime, hung in the doorway as we had no fireplace chimney. We found an orange and a piece of hard candy. Our parents did not emphasize Santa. We were encouraged to think of giving.

We both remembered helping our mother make stuffed toys for the Nebraska Children's Home a number of years. We sewed and stuffed tiny toy animals from material scraps we had. We thought the orphanage children less fortunate than us would enjoy little toys. One time our mother encouraged the neighbor ladies to sew for the children's home. We had a good time wrapping stuffed toys to be mailed to Omaha.

An early gift when I was five was a pink sweater to wear with a little paid skirt our mother made. I liked the sweater and felt confident to speak my first piece at night. Our Mom and Dad were in the back holding baby brother with two younger brothers. Older brother and sister pushed me out from behind the green burlap curtains. I looked at the crowd and got stage fright! I grabbed my skirt and covered my face and spoke my piece loud and clear. It was probably muffled by the skirt. I have no idea what the recitation was but no one will let me forget my first presentation. My sister said, "I was so embarrassed and mortified."

Years later I found a letter Mom had sent to Aunt Maud: "We have a new baby boy. He is a good baby. Beth has memorized her recitation for the school program though I don't know if she will say it. Teddy needs new shoes." There were comments on each child. I know I did my part for that Christmas program.

Christmases renew memories of singing Christmas songs and a live nativity in our lantern lit country school. Each student participated and went home feeling like we helped make the world better. I liked my piece the year I borrowed my sister's doll and Arlene's doll to place them on a bench to recite to. Our mother made new doll clothes to cover the well worn legs and head of my doll. She was busy with many responsibilities so I was impressed.

Hans and Christina Larsen's land joined ours so Dad and Mr. Larsen often fixed fence together. Mr Larsen told our folks he was repairing fence near our home when he heard chattering as Ted and I walked to school "to meet Lila and Jim." Mr. Larsen had a field of rye that we shocked as a family on our way to visit them. Dad stood bundles of grain up as we children carried them to him. I felt good about being a part of a family effort. Mr. Larsen bought a gun from Grandpa Paine's estate sale for Jim. I remember their kitchen bay window filled with old Christmas catalogs that we loved to look through.

COUNTRY PROGRESS

My parents, grandparents and great grandparents lived 50 miles from any medical facility. We rarely went anywhere except to school and school events. Roads were crooked, rough, seldom traveled, sandy trails from wagon or car tracks. We raised fruit and vegetables. Neighbors helped butcher beef or pork. Chickens laid eggs and provided meat.

Grandma Weber drove while Granddaddy, who had broke his arm, held their twin girls. Dad and his Grandpa sat in the back of their old rattly jitney to find a doctor when my dad broke his collar bone. He felt every bump of the twisty rough road. Most illnesses were cured by home remedies. Grandma Paine greased our necks with Menthol and wrapped them with our long cotton stockings on cold winter nights.

There was no telephone, running water or inside plumbing. Dad rode his horse to attend high school, traveling nine miles each way for 9nth grade. His 13 year old brother drowned in the lake north of their house. Lewis is buried on the ranch near infant brother, Samuel and sister, Pauline.

We put up hay with pitchforks and horses as a family. Hay was mowed by pulling a five foot mower. Horses pulled a dump rake to gather hay. We helped put up hay each summer. Windmills provided the water for livestock and family. Adults had a strong faith and shared with family and neighbors. My mother said she didn't like scatter raking because horses balked at going over the ground a second time. I didn't mind it driving a tractor wherever there was hay.

We teenagers, Jim, Ted and I, were delighted when the highway twelve miles away from our home was completed. We then had oil road to Thedford. We could stay home and drive every day for high school. Our parents paid for us to board with local families on stormy nights or game nights. We knew what it was like to stay far from home and not get home for months. We were thankful for privileges our parents didn't have.

In the fall of 1953 the Rural Electric came, putting in poles and wire into our house. We excitedly ran through the house turning on lights to see what a difference the electric bulbs made. Grandma Weber got a refrigerator. She said, "You will want cool milk." Our telephone was installed later that fall; it was a wall phone with a crank, hanging above the kitchen table. Our ring, five shorts, made us listen. We rarely had talked on a phone before. We survived and grew strong. It took hard work, long hours, a loving home environment, commitment of family and strong faith. We were survivors.

BEST FRIENDS

When I was little, my best friend was my sister, Lila, three years older than me. I admired and looked up to her for wisdom and guidance. We were happy playmates and I admired her abilities as the spokesperson for us. Jim, Ted, Glen, Gene and I would shyly stand peeking from behind our mother's skirt. We were content to let her answer questions for all of us.

Dad's youngest sisters, twin aunts, Flora and Florence, were playmates. They were a three years older than Lila. We greatly admired them and our close relationship in the family. We didn't have close neighbors but visited with aunts and grandparents often. Flora still calls often.

When I graduated from the 8th grade I began writing to a pen pal Eileen who lived near Streater, Illinois. She became a fun confidant. We began after I had written a letter to a newspaper requesting pen pals. Many answered and wrote for a time. Several continued writing a number of years. Eileen and I exchanged letters during high school and beyond. We have met and enjoyed ourselves twice. We felt like we'd always known each other. We still communicate via e-mail.

In Alma High School, Joy was my closest friend. Joy was an outgoing, fun girl to be around and a band majorette. Marilyn, Gail, Mildred, and Delia were friends and exchanged pictures. They were in band. I spent the most time with Lila and cousins Ruth Ann and John because we went to church and youth meetings together with Alyce, Darrell, Wendel and others. John and I were in band so rode the bus for trips and waited for his father to pick us up.

My closest friend in Gandy was Lucy. I liked Arleta, Mary Jane, Charlotte and Darlene. Lucy and I double dated and continued to keep in contact. She married Darrell, a second cousin, and moved away. We exchanged letters and pictures and still write or talk on the telephone.

Camp Witness and Maranatha Bible Camp offered opportunities to meet new friends. Some of my contacts were Betty,

June, Esther, Lois Jean, and Irene. I taught Bible School with some of the girls.

When highway 83 was completed my brothers, Jim, Ted and I were thankful to be able to live at home and drive an hour to school every night and morning. I enjoyed my brothers and glad to get home for supper, though late— after sports practices. (There were no sports for girls.) I welcomed the opportunity to visit with my mother while helping with dishes each evening. It was wonderful to be able to share about activities, concerns and joys with my mother and dad. (Before that we depended on weekly letters to communicate.)

My best friends in Thedford were classmates: Carolyn, Eleanor, Rose and Wanda. I studied, stayed over night and double dated with them. We practiced cheers so spent lots of time together. Wanda was the studious one but a fun person.

When I boarded in town as a senior I roomed with Jeannie who I called my 'Little Sis.' I was friends with the Florea daughters: Hazel, Mary Ann and Laura Bell. We got along fine. Their young niece Jacky followed me and I enjoyed her. My high school friends, Jacky and I walked to school together on frosty or on nice mornings. I was blessed to know who admired me. I had a reason to do what was right. "Everyone has an admirer," my mother often said, "so we need to be sure we do what is good to be a good role model." Thanks Jacky, for supporting what I did at school and at your Grandma and Grandpa Florea's home.

I felt left out when Wanda began talking to my roommate, Jeanne a lot every day one spring. On a windy cold afternoon, Carolyn drove in and said, "Come ride with me to Wanda's house for some supplies." I said, "No, she hasn't been talking to me lately so I won't impose." Carolyn talked a long time until I finally said I'd ride with her but not go inside. "I will wait for you in the car." Wanda came bouncing out to greet me. I learned then that Wanda was planning a surprise birthday party. She was trying to figure a way to get me to her home without spilling the plans. Our classmates were there and Wanda had baked a cake for Doris, her sister, and I who shared our birthday.

In college I was friends with Margaret, who I had met at Camp Witness Bible Camp. We studied elementary education and attended youth groups. My roommate, Jean was good support and I enjoyed time with her. We shared good times, studying and taking care of one another doing student teaching and the flu epidemic. She had/has a great sense of humor. We studied together and shared and are still friends; I check her mother, at 101 years, and report to Jean. I brought breakfast rolls to Betty Lou; she didn't get up. Lyn, a Thedford graduate, was a friend of Jane, my first roommate. Getha, Jan, Florence, Maxine, Manijeh, Fay, Nellie and Kathy were friends. I student taught with Deloris and Helen.

As an adult my closest friend and confidant was my husband Harold, for nearly 33 years of marriage. Then suddenly he was gone—a heart attack! My friends, Carolyn, Angeline and Marge and others were good moral support. I was busy farming. Shari helped me train for Extension work. She drove me to training sessions and helped write grants for Kids Team and projects. I don't know how I would have managed during those very long lonesome winters without her positive encouragement. She gave me hope for better days—until she was gone with cancer. Several years later, I met Jeanette who talked, served and prayed with me. She and I went places, cut each other's hair and enjoyed visiting. We were comfortable communicating until she had heart problems and died. Leora was a trusted friend with whom I could visit, study and pray. Her cancer death left another hole in my life. My special friends were encouraging through the years.

Margaret, Jean, Eileen, Lucy, Carolyn, Eleanor, Rose and Wanda are still in contact. My family is my strongest support system. My daughter is my friend and confident. My sons are just a phone call away and I am truly thankful for them. My brothers and sister call and share family news. Grandchildren still and always will bring special joy. They are a bright spot when they call or visit. God sends those we need in our lives for a time when we most need them. As years pass we move on. I trust He knows what is best for us every day. He has given me special friends through the years for which I am thankful.

COUNTRY LIVING

Sandhills living was challenging. When I announced to my parents, I wanted to graduate from college, my father scoffed, "Why would you want to go to college?" Parents discouraged girls from college, believing girls do not need higher education. I taught a rural school at 18 and saved my money, because I was determined to graduate from college. I wanted my parents to be there when I did. I did and they came in 1958 and again in 1988. I worked hard to earn the needed credits.

Rural families are rooted deep in the country, living near their children, grandchildren and great grandchildren as much as possible living in rural areas. My Mother's grandparents lived in the south central Nebraska beginning in 1881. They established ranches, raised families and livestock. Their descendants keep in contact. Good land stewards improve their land to leave it better than they found it.

Neighbors got together for meals and good times after harvest time or for 4th of July picnics. Families bonded for work and fun during hard times. We gathered to visit and celebrate special times. Especially memorable were when our soldier uncles came home on leave from the military. The last day of school was usually a fishing day. People put ice under straw and dirt and gathered neighbors to share ice cream making and eating. This was before electricity, ice boxes, refrigerators or inside plumbing.

Cooking was done on a wood range which held a reservoir for extra water. Water was carried from the windmill or pumped to heat for dish washing and laundry. Fresh water was in a bucket for drinking using a shared metal dipper. Branding and butchering meant families and neighbors gathered to help. Meat was shared with those helping.

CANOEING

Dad talked about taking a canoe ride on the Niobrara River west of Valentine and spoke of the idea for months. This wouldn't be a distant drive and, at 85, he thought the river ride would be great fun. He told stories he'd heard of friends' experiences gliding gracefully along the scenic rippling river waters. He was ready for a Niobrara River adventure.

When his birthday neared I made arrangements for myself and some friends to take him on a canoe ride on the Niobrara. We loaded his picnic box and set sail. Dad decided to sit on top of the picnic box 'for a better view.' Picturesque scenery was wonderful as we quietly canoed around big rocks, raises and curves in the river. We noticed rocks hidden amid the rippling water.

Rough water soon splashed and spilled into the canoe. Quickly the picnic box, on which Dad sat, slipped. The boat and Dad were suddenly tipped and plunged into fast moving water. I think Dad was glad that I was holding his camera in another canoe.

The strong water pushed Dad and the canoe fast backwards down the river. He was struggling and unable to get around the boat with the strong current. I jumped into the water and began pulling and tugging trying to hold the boat but I couldn't stop the boat either.

I called to an attractive young couple standing along the river bank, "Please help!" They looked like a couple from a movie with tanned shapely bikini clad bodies. They graciously stepped into the water and quickly pulled that canoe and helped my father ashore. I thanked them profusely and found they were from Omaha. By this time Dad got in and sat down quietly on the bottom of the canoe for the rest of his canoe trip down the Niobrara. He was exhausted from the scare and extra exertion.

When his pictures were developed, Dad called me. He seemed disappointed to find there were no pictures of him or the overturned boat. There wasn't time to think of snapping pictures at that moment.

Dad and I enjoyed looking over his pictures but he seemed disappointed that I hadn't taken any of the upside down canoe. He never again mentioned canoeing on the picturesque Niobrara River waters. I was on a Niobrara River canoe trip with a teacher education class many years later. My thoughts returned to Dad, remembering his birthday trip. The later river trip wasn't exciting as the trip with my Dad. The Niobrara River trip wore my father out but it certainly made memories.

COUNTRY CUTS

Country folks learn to make do. I feel good to have my hair trimmed. I began cutting hair when I was about 11 as my mother asked if I would trim her hair. She told me how she wanted it and I did it. I have been cutting hair ever since. I cut my mother's regularly and I started cutting my own shortly after. I've cut hair for many friends.

Living miles from neighbors or a town teaches country people to be resourceful; we took care of ourselves and our families. There was no support for women so we did extra jobs. My mother bought home permanents and cut and curled hair for my sister and me when we were little. Permanents left fine hair a bit too curly. When it rained my hair drooped. We tried to look our best. At a rainy track meet years ago we school girls all had kinky hair from permanents.

Neighbor cut and curled my hair then I figured I could do that myself. I felt good cutting my hair, my friends,' and mother's hair. Dad cut brother's hair for years using hand clippers.

Cutting my husband's hair began soon after our wedding. He came home with a bad haircut and asked if I could fix it. I cut his hair ever after. We found out his barber had lost his partner and was drinking. I gave my father-in-law and sons hair cuts for years. My husbands' uncle drove from town for a haircut. A neighbor asked Gramps, " Who cuts your hair?" That made him feel good about his haircut. I gave myself permanents - with my husband's help to neutralize, when I did it myself I found I missed some curls and it didn't hold. I appreciated his help. I've never charged for hair cuts. I heard it is against the law to charge to cut hair with no license. Cutting hair is a fun diversion offering an opportunity to visit.

I felt like crying when I first cut our little sons' hair. One had beautiful blond fine silky hair and the other had dark curls. The first hair cut meant our tiny boys were growing up. At six months, people began asking, "Is that a girl?" I felt I must trim his curls on the sides. Their Dad kindly suggested, "You better cut his curls for we don't want people to think he's a girl."

Friend Jeanette and I cut each other's hair for years and enjoyed our time together. She'd say, "Isn't it time we got together?" She carried sharp scissors in her purse for when we met. It was fun to look forward to snipping and visiting. She liked for me to drive to her house so she'd fix lunch to share as we worked or sewed and chatted.

Cutting hair is satisfying and enjoyable. When I feel a haircut might improve my state of mind, I get out my sharp scissors and head for a mirror. Snipping provides a way to lift my spirits. When I cut my hair, I think of Jeanette and my mother. They were my inspiration and encouragement for years. I still miss them.

SLEEPY AND A GUN

My mother spoke often of Sleepy, a shiny black horse that she rode to country school. She was young, in 1922, when a lone horseman rode in to their ranch home on a black, long legged, severely winded horse. The stranger offered to give his horse, saddle, bridle and pistol to Grandpa for a ride to the nearest railroad depot that day. My aunt reported, "Mom said the horse was so tired he slept for days."

"Papa was afraid of the man; he would not, in ordinary circumstances, have hitched up his horses and driven the team and wagon over 35 miles on trail roads in late afternoon to take him to the depot," she added. Our grandparents operated the Elizabeth Post Office and were accustomed to people riding in for mail but this man was different.

They had two daughters, my mother and the younger, my aunt, was two. She said they had Sleepy as long as she could remember. Grandpa was a quiet trusting gentleman, always thoughtful and protecting of his family. My aunt now 91, emphasized, "That rider struck fear in the heart of my father! The man had a gun that had recently been fired!" She added, "He seemed terribly nervous and wanted to get to the depot that night."

Our mother claimed the gentle worn out Sleepy as her horse. "He was a fine saddle horse and Irene rode him to school every day," my aunt added. "Irene was quite upset when she found Harvey O'Neil rode Sleepy hard one day." She said, "Irene and her friend Dora Smith rode their horses exploring the Sandhills. When Irene was too little to open gates she held up fence wires and Sleepy would go through."

My mother told me she rode Sleepy around the neighbors' lake west of them, when Lewis drowned in May 1923. When it was cold and stormy, my mother said she wrapped her long dark braids around her ears for protection from wind and gave Sleepy his reins to run home on a lope. "Sleepy ran directly to the barn door," she reported. Later Aunt Mildred rode Sleepy to school and raced him with her classmate, Dot. "Sleepy never lost a race." she happily exclaimed. The gun, COLT 25 pistol #53685, made in Hartford, Connecticut, was patented, August 25, 1897 is in possession of my aunt. She offered it to me then said, "It is old and rusted with the trigger stuck," I had not seen the gun so cousin Judy sent a picture of the Colt 25. The old pistol resurrects memories for our family, a well bred trained running horse named Sleepy, a stranger and Grandpa protecting his family by taking a stranger to the Wood Lake Rail Road Station at night. Sleepy is part of our family legacy.

ELECTRICITY

Electricity and telephone came to us the fall of 1953 while Jim, Ted and I were in high school in Thedford. Lila was teaching nearby. We came home Friday night, looked around wide-eyed, noticing lights in our house were brilliant!

A refrigerator was in the kitchen. We tried every light to see how bright the rooms were. Mama was looking forward to making ice cream without a crank on the freezer. Soon we had running water and a bathroom. (That fall a visiting minister's wife asked me outside where our outhouse was. She didn't know we had running water and an inside bathroom. Rev and Mrs. Hollingshead remembered when we didn't have running water or electricity.)

Dad bought our mother a toaster. Next came an electric washing machine, mixer and a dryer. Her treadle sewing machine was replaced with an electric model. She marveled in her last years when I bought a computer and learned to use it.

We lived in Cherry County and my father lived all his life there, 50 miles south-east of Valentine and 40 miles north-west of Thedford, our closest town. Our mail carrier, a link to the world, came to our box three times a week. We went to school and back home. There were plenty of chores: picking up cobs, carrying wood, getting in milk cows and feeding critters.

Our Dad drove a Ford pickup with parents and six kids crowded in the cab in winter to travel to school programs. He hung a lantern for school programs and carried a lantern to the barn to milk cows by hand, Dad laughed as he squirted us and the cats with fresh milk. Separated milk was on the porch to cool. Cream was shipped to Norfolk on the mail route. We helped churn cream into butter by shaking a quart jar. We had a turn churn later.

Dad had built a 32 volt battery system charger to provide the luxury of radio, which we had used sparingly for news. It was a treat to hear "The Grand Ole Opry" on Saturday nights if those batteries were up. We were around the breakfast table when the radio brought news of Pearl Harbor bombing and again when the first casualty in the county, our neighbor's son, was announced on our radio. We turned off all lights when there was a 'black out.' It was scary to think of the need for a black out that far out but we obeyed and shut off all lights.

The 32 volt system provided dim lights through bare light bulbs with a string attached, suspended in the middle of each room. Many evenings were spent with the motor running to charge those 32 batteries which became dim after a few hours use.

Our grandparents lived in sod houses lit with lamp light for years. We witnessed progress from pumping our water to digging a cistern for running water. We learned to appreciate bright lights, running water and an inside toilet and a real bathtub.

The little round galvanized bathtub became a memory, as did the outside privy, thunder jugs, kerosene lamps and other old ways. I joined my family being thankful to be "turned on."

COUNTRY FAMILY

When I think back of my family, my parents, sister and four brothers, I realize now how blessed we were. We didn't have material things and they weren't important - people were and still are. We had caring parents who worshiped God and respected others. Shouldn't anyone respect and honor a parent who kept their word and do what is right? We ate on cracked plates but we didn't mind. I wore cotton dresses, mostly hand downs from sister or aunts or feed sack ones my grandma or mother made.

Our parents did not demonstrate love with hugs and kisses. Thinking about it now, I believe they were trying to avoid any appearances of being improper. They showed they cared by demonstrating an interest and involvement in our activities. We went to town crowded in Dad's old black Ford pickup over bumpy rough country trail roads. When there were rural school parties, county wide school music or school track meets we were there even if it was inconvenient. They organized a 4-H club, Sunday School to help us learn, to set goals and to meet other young people.

I found about Camp Witness at Long Pine and Dad took Ted, Glen and me. He came after us with all the family. I learned a lot and met some wonderful friends. I began teaching Bible School in the summers as a teen ager. I learned as well as the students I taught. I was teaching north of Mullen when Mom called to say Great Grandmother had passed away. I had promised to teach at Elsmere the following week so I missed her memorial service. I felt she would have approved, for she had organized the Sunday School in Elsmere years earlier.

Our mother prepared plain nourishing meals, morning, noon and night for sit down family meals together. We had meat, potatoes and vegetables, fresh when available. We gathered around the table to eat together. Breakfast included oat meal, unless Daddy came in and helped. He made pancakes, French toast, or fried eggs and bacon. There was conversation and respect between our parents and us. When Jim, Ted and I drove to Thedford the last two years of my high school, supper was waiting when we got home. It was late but our folks waited. The food tasted good. Afterwards, I helped my mother with dishes and discussed the days' activities. It was a blessing to be home. Other years we boarded away for high school and our mother wrote each week. At Uncle Albert's, he would ask, "What's new on the ranch?" Lila and I handed the letter to him to read which pleased him. He would comment on our Mother's news. It was far from home but we knew our parents were thinking of us.

On band trips, Uncle was waiting for the bus or a call telling him John and I were back. He drove carefully and never let us drive. A youth was hit in an accident on their railroad crossing so he was extremely cautious. We felt love and respect but it wasn't home. I longed for home in the country with our family where nights were so dark we could see stars and the moon. I appreciated home. That's where my heart leads— to a special bond of family and home.

MEASLES

Our parents brought home baby Gene Paul ten days after his December 8th birth in the Ainsworth hospital. We were excited to see our Mama and to hold 'our baby.' Mama soon came down with the hard red German measles, caught from her roommate's children. Children were allowed in hospitals to visit then. We went to see her, the only time we went to Ainsworth, while she was in the hospital. I cried to see her lying in bed. A short time later our baby brother was speckled all over with the measles. Mama showed his spotted back as she stripped him for his daily bath. She plastered his tiny body with soda to ease the uncomfortable spots. Grandma and Mama talked about the blotchy red spots on Gene. New babies are supposed to be immune from diseases their first several months.

Then the unthinkable happened: we siblings, ages two, four, five, six and eight, came down with the measles. Lila said she and Dad went to get Grandma and her rocking chair to come stay with us. Grandma came and helped care for the rest of us. My brothers and I lay together on the sofa bed, itching and scratching. The window was covered with a heavy quilt to keep out the bright sunlight reflecting on the snow. Our eyes hurt, food tasted terrible and we had head-aches. We were instructed to get up and come to the table for meals. We didn't have to eat but we were to show up. We did, even when we were feeling most miserable. I willingly bedded down under the warm covers where we stayed sleeping a lot. Jim thought they rubbed Vicks on itchy spots. Lila said, "Granddaddy Weber came and did the chores, feeding cattle, hogs and chickens plus milking cows and separating milk when Dad caught the measles."

Our baby recovered with tender loving care. Jim thought Dad and Lila caught the measles later, after he, Ted, Glen and I. One day our Mama came in and said, "Get up, you've been laying in bed long enough." We reluctantly folded the bedding and put the sofa back together.

Lila said we missed the Valentine's Day party at school because of the measles. Dad probably wasn't feeling up to driving us or maybe he still had spots from measles. I remember our mother's hands always felt cold. I believe her hands were cold because she didn't have a fever thermometer. She held her hands on our foreheads to check when we were feverish.

We were thankful to be over the measles. Then Gene caught the measles again, eleven years later. Our Mom was most unhappy. She thought it was enough that he had the measles as an infant. I felt bad for her, doctoring him with concern for measles again.

THE '49 BLIZZARD

Heavy snow began falling as a blizzard in mid December and continued blowing and drifting day after day. Pictures show trains stranded in deep snowdrifts. People were airlifted from remote homes. I remember our hills and meadows covered with a multiple deep drifts. We lived far from any neighbor or improved roads. Our folks kept supplies so we didn't worry about running out of food or necessities.

Daddy came to school for us younger ones with his horse pulling a small wooden cart. Mama sent warm blankets and scarves to wear in the wagon filled with hay. I tied a scarf around my neck and pulled it up over my face to endure the sharp stinging wind.

Our dad brought his cows home from the east pasture with a load of hay. He turned his cows to feed, sheltered beside the house. He promised Mama if they killed her favorite plants he would replace them. The cattle milled beside the house and stomped on everything. He kept his word to replant trees, flowers and shrubs in the well fertilized soil.

Lila was high school in Beatrice. Dad rode his horse to contact neighbor, Al Higgins who had a phone and his brother Don had an airplane in Ainsworth, to get her home. She rode a train to Ainsworth and flew home in an airplane which landed on our meadow. Dad made plans for her to return the same way, as roads were still not open. I snapped a picture of Lila and Gene standing on top of a tall yard post drifted over before she left for high school where she stayed with Grandma and Great Aunt Fannie. She was quarantined and embarrassed by chicken pox that winter.

Winds and snow made the hills look like a white frosted fairyland. Drifts covered tree tops and buildings. Daddy crawled out through a window to scoop a tunnel to the corral and chicken house to check on livestock and to chop firewood. Eggs were froze and pigs were under a deep drift in their shed. My brothers and I bundled in heavy coats, snow pants, scarves, mittens and high buckle overshoes to carry in arm loads of fire wood which Daddy chopped and split. I was part of the wood carrying team that our

Dad loaded in our open arms. We tramped into the house to pile the firewood high to keep the fires burning. When the sun came out we pulled a couple of little wooden sleds to the top of the tallest evergreen trees behind our Grandparent's home. My brothers and I enjoyed a long fun, but scary 'tree slide.' We slid rapidly on the pine treetops, then the snow melted and it was unsafe.

Mama and I watched out a frosty window as a small airplane circled our place and dropped several large bags of mail near our garden fence. Brothers and I ran outside to gather two big mail bags struggling beneath their weight. We received Christmas cards in late January in that mail bag. One bag was for our neighbors which Dad delivered on his horse, as communication was person to person.

Another day we heard a low flying airplane and watched as it dropped bales of hay for our neighbors' cattle in a grove of trees just south of us. Mom said we didn't need emergency hay. All of our roads were blocked and we had no way to move beyond the yard.

The National Guard 'weasels' came with huge plows to move snow making trail roads. Neighbors took turns feeding the weasel drivers warm meals and guiding them. Daddy was on a late night shift directing a driver. He came home the next morning covered with ice and snow telling stories of deep drifts they plowed around and through to make a path to the next place. He went 12 miles before returning home. By then it was morning and Mom had prepared a steaming hot breakfast of coffee, cereal, eggs and pancakes ready for our family, for Dad and the weasel driver. Over sixty years have passed and still we remember the '49 blizzard!

WORK AND FUN

Our parents kept busy doing worthwhile work. By nightfall they were bone weary but thankful for good health for themselves and their children. Lila became a veracious reader after getting glasses. She collected books she liked reading through the years.

Chickens were raised for home use and their extra eggs were sold for sometimes six cents a dozen. We had beef and pork to eat at butchering time. Neighbors rallied to help; fresh liver was carried inside to wash, cool in water and to share with the helpers.

Mom canned beef to preserve for winter. Pork was salted, cured or canned. She boiled cracklings for lard. Hogs were hard work to feed and confine. They were hauled to town and sold for four cents a pound. Dad went to town for feed and often took a hog to sell for cash. We helped unload corn. Chickens sold for four cents a pound; we ate ours. They were tasty with dumplings or noodles. Fresh made corn bread or bread were yummy. Milk fresh was for drinking and separating for the cream to sell. Gas cost 15 cents a gallon. Cows were milked twice a day. Cats waited patiently for a squirt of fresh milk. We children watched. We tried squeezing milk from the cows. It is harder than it looked and takes time to learn. Cows can and do kick.

Our parents were loving grandparents. When Dad was alone he enjoyed his great grandchildren. They loved him. Two year olds, Ashley and Tyler fought swatting one another, telling each other, "No, that's my great grandpa!" They didn't know Grandpas are shared. Memories of long ago linger for reminiscing.

QUILTS TIE FAMILIES

Quilts tie families together. Our ancestors carried quilts in covered wagons. An 1847 quilt appliquéd, with initials and date, is priceless though ragged. My sister and I grew up sleeping under a Sunbonnet Girls quilt made by Grandma Paine. Material was carefully cut from scraps of our dresses and the boys shirts. That quilt is thread-bare but a reminder of Grandma's love and caring.

Log Cabin and Jacobs Ladder print patterns were of heavy dark quilts. On cold nights we slept under comfortable old tied quilts made of dark heavy square blocks from old coats. Dresden Plate and appliquéd Rose pattern quilts made by Great Grandmother Giles were given to my sister and me. A note on one says the small white material pieces in the back were left over scraps of gowns made for military hospitals during World War I.

An early memory is tying a quilt of dark heavy squares on a frame in our living room the day Glen was born. Ted and I, almost three and four, "helped" beneath the quilt, pushing a big needle up through the material.

Grandma Paine made Flower Garden quilts hand stitched of bright material for her four granddaughters. She carried material, thimble, needle and thread with her when she traveled to visit. She laid out blocks on the floor to make pleasing arrangements. She machine sewed quilts for grandsons. Glen's was turquoise and white diamond shapes for an heirloom keepsake.

Our Mama loved quilts and embroidered a delicate pink flower quilt while attending Chadron College and offered it to me in college. I felt good to use that quilt on my bed. She made quilts for her grandchildren. A memorable quilt Mom made was for Grandma Weber for her 80th birthday of traced hand prints and appliquéd blocks of each great grandchild, with blue cuffs for boy's and lacy cuffs for the girls.

Jerry and Wayne were in high school when we cut blocks of denim and red flannel for their quilts. Kristi requested a quilt so I painted animal pictures for her. I machine stitched cat screen print blocks that I made in college of a picture I took of our cat sitting on the barn door. I began quilting for grandchildren when there were five. I've made seven quilts but there's more and I'm far behind. I have begun on the eighth quilt plus little ones for the great grandchildren.

For our parent's 40th anniversary, I wrote names and dates of them, their grandparents and parents, then I drew and painted red roses for their children and spouses plus twelve grandchildren with birthdays. The great grandchildren were on rosebuds.

I requested family members to decorate a block of shared memories for our parent's 50th anniversary. A favorite was a block showing inside the governors' mansion of an over sized table under an imported chandelier with cat tracks. I drew a picture of my folk's three legged dog and his paw. Flora drew a honey jar. There was an interesting variety of pictures.

Andy and I shopped to choose a John Deer pattern. He packed his quilt for college. Ten year old Joey got sick so my friend Jeanette helped me make his Eagle quilt and a matching pillow. He smiled sweetly and said, "I like my quilt and I use it every day." Will choose a colorful chicken print with bright green on the back. He was delighted and quipped, "My quilt looks even nicer than I thought it would." He was cheerful inspecting his quilt. Cody selected wild animal material with a blue background. He was pleased with his quilt. Ashley hesitated so I found a bright colored print of cats and birds for her quilt with pale blue and white pattern in alternate blocks. She seemed happy holding her quilt for a picture.

Mindy has a patriotic red, white and blue patterned quilt reminding me of how striking she looked in her patriotic naturalization dress. Ana's quilt is brightly framed cat and bird blocks. She smiled sweetly for her quilt picture. Alyssa requested a princess pattern quilt of lavender. Her Princess quilt is simple but not finished. Ivan liked all the quilt pictures. He and I will check material. Ben may wait awhile. Marina and Jade will keep me quilting.

I appliquéd baby quilt for my great grandson, Carson Wayne in Germany. Great grandson, Joseph Ronald has his baby quilt and Addie Nichole got hers. Quilts are stitched to create a legacy of love. I have a pictures of each grandchild holding their quilt. Quilts really do tie families together like Ted and I helped tie our mother's quilts years ago.

QUILTS

Quilts are made of material and thread
That is so very true
Each one is carefully stitched with
patience, caring and love too
Love holds the tired hands steady
When you want to quit
Love reminds us of threads we knit
When you see a unique quilt

Memories flood our creative senses
There is baby's first shirt
And tiny dresses, I do recall
Baby quilts are little and delicate

Quilts stitched with material and thread
Stitched with love expectation
Our future is alive with our past
And great anticipation.

SETTING GOALS

A goal of mine was to see England where Grandma and her older siblings were born. Grandma Paine had a faded postcard picture of the church and the door of their home. She talked of Brompton where they had lived. I wanted to see it. I thought for years I would take Grandma to England. She was two when they left so it would have been a thrill for her.

When Grandma got older, she broke her hip which ended ideas of her traveling. I talked about taking my mother and then my daughter to England. My mother broke her hip and my daughter got married and had a baby so traveling to England seemed far in the future. Was it time to take that trip?

I got my passport, made arrangements to fly across the ocean. I saw the huge old church in Brompton, England where the little Vasey children were christened in 1881 when our Grandma was two weeks. I saw an altar where their parents were married December 16, 1849.

Seeing inside the church was a thrill beyond imagination to me. There were individual decorated kneeling benches in every pew. I had looked at the pictures my grandma had in faded sepia and tried to imagine them in color. I asked Grandma many questions and she was glad to talk about what she had heard from her mother years before.

My dream came true on March 17, 2004 driving to Denver Airport and leaving exactly 123 years after Grandma's birth. The flight was long and tiring landing in Manchester, England where Grandma's mother Margaret Agnes Tindale was born. I visited other travelers asking questions. Some had heard of the Vasey name, "There is a comedian by that name." He was a big rough talker, a man told me. No one knew of the little town of Brompton. I found the very old church and home looked just like Grandma's pictures. Ebberston where Grandma's grandparents lived and were married was three miles away, with a town between. I walked around both churches and talked to some residents.

I met a friendly researcher in Brompton and a lady named Daphne Vasey in Ebberston. We compared notes and found our ancestral lines matched with the same names, George and Mary (Bernette) Vasey married on May 1,1770 in St. Mary's Church in Ebberston. She showed me the Vasey Coat of Arms. We took pictures and enjoyed visiting. I asked if she is diabetic and she said, "No but my sister is!" We decided we are related.

I walked around the churches, inside and out taking pictures. I had my picture taken by the very large Brompton church door. There are huge tomb stones around the courtyard. The above ground tomb beside the door is dated 1703. I found stones with "Vasey." I scratched off centuries' accumulation of moss with my keys. I bought postcards of the church, in color! I walked around a pond taking pictures with the big picturesque church in the background. Beautiful ducks and swans swam and nested nearby. The wind blew strong as I continued walking and taking pictures—mostly of the church. The church in different angles and lights was impressive even when the sky turned rainy and dark. The last day I said, "I want to see Brompton and Ebberston once more."

Eating lunch in the Brompton pub across the street from the Post Office, the only eating place in the town, was fun. I met the nicest people and asked many questions. A man, celebrating his 77th birthday, invited us to stay with him in Scarborough, 'if you ever return.' When we left, after exchanging addresses, he kissed my cheek and said how pleased he was to meet someone from America. "You are the second person I've met from America," he exclaimed.

The Vasey family home was on a street with lots of other homes built together. The Vasey house had the door painted dark green. Across the street was like a park. I didn't walk across but wish I had. Dirt streets were long and narrow. Cousin Joan later learned, the castle where Great Grandmother Margaret lived with her grandparents was in Brompton and has disappeared but there was a hill above the edge of town called Castle Hill.

Letters Great Grandmother Margaret wrote to my Grandma in 1909 said, "The old castle was in ruins" when she, George, brothers, Frank and Dowsland and wife returned. They were glad they had sailed across the ocean but by the end of the trip Margaret was ready to return to her children and home in America. I believe I understand her feelings. I will always be glad I saw England where my Grandma was born and talked about for years. Now I can share stories about Brompton with my children and my grandchildren. I have pictures, souvenirs and memories to share about visiting England.

Gramps and Grandma Gibbons holding little Wayne, with two year old, Jerry, standing beside them.

SEWING

Our cheerful white haired Grandmas were the best when it came to innovative gift giving. I don't believe they missed a birthday or Christmas with a card and note or gift they made. I was little but I vividly remember seeing Grandma with her white hair braided and twisted on top her head, sewing on her treadle sewing machine with a paper pattern for a white muslin cow and pig. She used the old treadle sewing machine then did hand stitching to close the stuffed critter and shell coverings.

The idea for the animals was the same but coverings were red polka dot material for the cow and soft pink for a lop eared pig for youngest brothers. Grandma included me to help stuff the cuddly critters. She explained challenges and encouraged me to 'help.' She laughed as we worked. Grandma was living with us so she used whatever material she had and sewed for everyone. She put the basic critter inside the covering so it was removable for washing yet durable enough for little boys play. She used black embroidery floss to hand stitch their funny features: eyes, nose and mouth. Brothers carried their animals around for years. They'd ask, "Where is Pig?" or "Have you seen Cow?"

Grandma made cow and pig for 1942. Christmas for Glen and Gene. I know, for I found an old picture of "Pig" and Glen with a big smile taken the following spring. I am thankful my mother wrote names and dates on pictures so there is no doubt of who, what, where and when. When he came to visit I gave him the picture plus Pig. He said he would share Pig with his teenage grandchildren. I hope they cherish memories of their Great Grandma and Grandpa as they relive the time a special pig maker long ago spent hours creating that pig. Bygone days are important in our memories. Children need to share information to bring closeness like we had long ago, when life was simpler and days were filled with shared activities. Our grandmas took care to do a neat job of sewing, laughing as they worked. They reworked old clothes of Mildred's, the twins or Lila's for me. A fuzzy soft coat and muff were ones I remember wearing. Years later, Mildred painted an acrylic picture from the photograph of me wearing that coat and muff made of her old coat. Some clothes seemed like they'd been around too many times.

A MEMORABLE CHRISTMAS

A fun memorable Christmas was when my two little grandsons came running through the old farm kitchen door carrying a big white fuzzy 'kitten.' Closer inspection of 'kittens' revealed the little boys were holding kitten slippers for my Christmas. I loved those little boys and their gifts! They had plenty of hugs and big smiles to share besides slippers.

Those little guys each had the biggest smiles and were so proud of themselves to be giving such a wonderful gift to one they loved. Years later this gift affords continued happiness in my memory bank of special times. These precious little boys were doing what they liked most, giving to their Grandma.

When my father came to visit, he came out of the bedroom wearing the biggest grin carrying a slipper. His eyes twinkled as he laughed and said, "I found a cat under my bed!" I keep those fuzzy slippers as a soft reminder of happy times past. The cat slippers rest beside my bed so I can bask in the feeling of love and cheerfulness, with the memories they invoke, when I slip my feet into them on cold winter mornings. Those fuzzy slippers were truly a thoughtful gift to make a memorable Christmas and good memories for the years that follow.

WATER

When I was little, Lila and I made 'onion tea' on hot summer days. This was water with a little salt and a bunch of cut up onion tops added. We enjoyed drinking this onion tea while playing outside. Our table was a wooden box we shared. Lila learned to make this from our grandmothers and we enjoyed drinking this with brothers. The drink was good for making anyone want more water. Old timers were brilliant to figure what was good for themselves and their families. They didn't write their recipes but they shared what they knew.

I carry a water bottle with me to refill often but I do not get the recommended water to drink daily. Our family didn't drink coffee, except Dad had a cup of strong coffee so strong that we his children did not pick up the habit. It upset my stomach when I tried it. There are multiple benefits from drinking plenty of water daily. Water helps us replace excess fat and we feel more satisfied without eating so much. Summer heat makes us need to drink more water. Our mother encouraged us to get a drink of water whenever we thought we were hungry or uneasy. Sandhill water was pure and good for us.

COMFORT FOOD

Cold winter days, when the wind in blowing and snow is falling bring on winter blahs then it is time to bake. My mother often made an easy, delicious, date bread during November and December. She and I baked several loaves at a time. Some were frozen while others were sliced and eaten fresh. She would bring ice cream to top the date bread. Date bread is a taste treat with or without a topping.

My mother-in-law baked a similar recipe during winter months with a topping that was rich and delicious. It was to what you could call 'sinfully delicious.' She was a good cook who loved to prepare special recipes for holidays.

A favorite memory is of carrying suitcases getting loaded into the old tan 1949 Studebaker with brother Jim for the return trip to college. Our Mom hurried back inside saying, "Wait a minute." She came out with her tasty date bread slices. Those thin nutty date slices were wonderful. We ate together enjoying every bite; then she packed some in a sack to eat when we got hungry along the 200 mile trip to our dormitory. This long ago memory lingers with a mouth watering toasty comfortable warm feeling.

MOM'S DATE BREAD

1 cup sugar

1 egg

1 Tablespoon shortening 1

½ cups flour

½ teaspoon baking powder

½ cup nuts

1 ½ pound dates

1 cup boiling water

1 teaspoon soda

Pour boiling water over dates and let set in pan. Mix ingredients in bowl. Dissolve dates in water by using a fork/hands, mix them with the dry ingredients, shortening and egg. Stir and put into two loaf pans. Bake at 300 degrees for 45 minutes. Slice and enjoy. Topping: ½ pound dates, ½ cup nuts, ½ cup water. Boil until thick. Serve over top of thin Date Bread slices. This is a delicious recipe for when you are entertaining.

REMEDIES

Old remedies are proven successful daily. A professor proved his grandmothers' chicken and vegetable soup really do help cure colds and make sick people better. My parents were practical; they rarely went to a doctor. Daddy went to Ainsworth for an appendicitis operation when I was one. They knew when they needed professional help.

Our parents lined us up after breakfast in the cold winter seasons for a healthy dose of Cod Liver Oil. Our mother went down the line giving us each a teaspoon full of oil from a big bottle. We took it many cold mornings. It seemed like we had to take lots of the evil tasting stuff. I know we all used the same spoon as they delivered the 'medicine.'

We didn't dare disobey or challenge this ritual. We obediently did what our parents asked then coughed and/or gagged. We stood with opened mouths like little sparrows gulping down the horrible tasting stuff trying not to choke. We made terrible faces each time. I'm not sure how much good the Cod Liver Oil did. We survived and grew up becoming healthy adults. Haven't heard if Cod liver oil is still around for medicines.

My parents continued traditions of home remedies. We used salt and soda to brush our teeth. Soda was a remedy for an upset stomach. Turpentine was used for open cuts or sores. We washed infections and soaked in hot Lysol water, as hot as we could stand. Mama was a believer in applying a hot wash cloth to sores. A cold cloth was used to stop bleeding, soothe bruises or help relieve headaches. A cool cloth works wonders. I follow the cool cloth routine.

To disinfect a broken blister, add a few drops of Listerine for a powerful antiseptic. Vinegar heals bruises just soak a cotton ball in white vinegar and apply to bruises for an hour. Vinegar reduces bruised color and speeds up the healing process.

Skunk oil, lard or goose grease were remedies for aches and pains. This was for a home made liniment. Rub liberally on sore muscles. We used hot dry cloths with Vicks rubbed on our chest and throat. We breathed Vicks when we had the croup at nights. I remember listening to my youngest brother breathe easier after inhaling Vicks vapors. Our Grandma P was a great believer in wearing night caps and a long stocking around our necks at night. She made flannel night caps for us.

Old remedies work wonders. Grandma always used a bit of vinegar mixed with water to rinse her hair and ours. It makes your hair 'squeaky clean.' She encouraged taking a mixture of honey and vinegar when you feel a sore throat coming. Just mix 1/4 cup of vinegar with 1/4 cup of honey and take one tablespoon six times a day. Vinegar kills bacteria.

Cover skin blemishes with a dab of honey and place a Band aid over them. Honey kills the bacteria, keeps the skin sterile and speeds healing overnight. When my brother cried with an earache our mother came upstairs bringing a warm cloth for him to hold on his ear. She heated oil for a dropper when he continued hurting.

A mosquito repellent was a paste of vinegar and salt placed on unprotected skin for mosquitoes. Our mother put soda on mosquito bites after they'd been accosting us. We didn't put vinegar and salt on before going outside. Probably we didn't because it would have been a struggle to keep up with all of us during the summer months. We ran inside and out circulating around our home place continuously. Our parents reinforced the idea of wearing clothing to cover our arms and legs to prevent excess exposure to mosquitoes.

Our grandparents' wisdom came from experience and was handed down through the generations. My father-in-law had more remedies in his bank of wisdom than I had heard of before. He was a wise gentleman. The good thing about these remedies was they worked then and they still do!

I am thankful for knowledge of the old remedies.

Back row: Kristi, Wayne and Jerry holding Will. Sitting in front: Cody, Joe and Andy holding Ashley in summer of 1992.

PANHANDLE LIFE

LITTLE COWBOYS

Growing up in the country was a happy time for our little sons. They wanted to "be a cowboy just like Daddy." They wore cowboy boots and were proud of their felt hats. I made western shirts with pearl snaps and original fancy yokes sewed with decorative stitching. They rode their ponies bareback to attend rural school for eight years. They were real little cowboys.

Young cowboys rode to school and home. Their father said riding bareback was the safest. He rode to school bareback for eight years. Our boys trotted on their ponies taking off bridles and keeping ponies in a shed at school after feeding and watering them. They enjoyed riding but were glad to give the ponies their rein to head home at an easy lope.

Their father and mother and grandparents rode horses to school so a family tradition continues. When I was little we carried lunch bags our mother made for us, with a strap over our shoulders, for food, towel and cup. The only accident through the years riding our big horse to school was when gentle Rusty jumped at a gate breaking the cinch. Sister broke her arm, I landed on my head and brother Ted, in front of the saddle, was left straddling the horse.

Boots were important gifts when our boys were small. Cowboy hats were practical, they shaded their eyes and looked like Daddy. We thought we had the cutest cowboys. Cowboys grew up to find jobs and work serving their families and employers.

Grandsons: Andy, Will, Cody and Joey were cowboys from the beginning. They liked wearing boots and western hats. They rode horses and learned to control them. Cody wore a cowboy duster to county fair at four and rode his horse in local parades. When they visited, they rode these ponies they loved, sometimes two or three on one horse.

I prayed for protection of our little cowboys when they rode horses at home and when riding as teenagers. Children are special to parents and grandparents. I prayed when Cody was a wrangler at Fort Robinson. Twice a week the wranglers put on a 'cowboy rodeo' for tourists. He rode a bucking horse and enjoyed leading tourists on trail rides. His picture leading ride was in a Nebraskaland pamphlet.

Andy is now working using the computer skills he learned in Mitchel, South Dakota college. Will is taking college classes walking on Canadian crutches since an accident at 16. Doctors had said Will may never walk again but our Will is strong willed enough to prove them wrong. Joey is watching from Heaven's gate after a hard fought battle with brain stem cancer. Sergeant Cody served in Iraq and Germany to protect our country. He is now in National Guard and college. Cody took his western hat, jeans and boots as they represented US on foreign soil.

Grandmas do not forget to write and to pray for families and service people throughout the world. Cowboys grow up to protect their families. They set an example while working for peace around the world. Ashley and her mother also ride horses and enjoy the outdoors.

Horses in my pasture belong to grandchildren who ride when they have time from school or work. The tradition of riding horses creates a bond in rural families. Cowboys and cowgirls have working ranch and farm families to emulate.

CALENDAR ENTRIES OF OUR FIVE YEAR OLD

Do you suppose Aunt Deann weighs a ton or half a ton?

I want to tell you something that's not important. What do centipedes do?

Your eyes must have 'eyephorpebia.' That pink skirt kind of embarrasses me.

Are you sure how many legs a centipede has? This cloth insorbs best.

Dad said Prince looks up when he says oats; he looks up when you say fence pliers too. I tried it. There's a rock called Aunt Bestes. (asbestos)

Spot, you leave my bone alone! (He had been carrying a bone he claimed in his pocket.)

My corn is all castled. (tasseled) What's all the combersation about?

How much blood is in a person? I'm panting because it's so hot.

I found an injured cricket. (at 3 a.m.) I want a sandwich. Anything I can do for you?

You know what I call misery, going to more than one place in a day.

Mom, why don't you put on a pretty dress? I'll show you which one it is.

Mom, Cute has a cavity. I opened her mouth. (Cute is our cat)

I'm going to operate on this grass hopper. Shall we clean here and make a neat mess?

Do men ever marry girls older than them? Well, Gramps didn't. Daddy didn't. I can figure. Didn't you think I could figure? (He has always been good at math figuring.)

There's four orphan grasshoppers on my sunflowers. (albino.)

Who is the richest person in Nebraska? Probably Aunt or Uncle or the Game Permission. Would you like a 'mote control car? Why do you waste yourself changin' it?

How am I ever going to get all my color books colored?

Another place to write down to see is Mt. Fugi. It's in Asia and I'd like to see it.

How old was I when you got married? I'm going to get married when I'm six or 12.

How long have Gramps and Grandma been married? I hope they make it to your 100th.

(After hearing that Peggy Sue said she'd just go live with us) Don't you think she'd be a nuisance in our house? It's such a tiny cup, I can hardly get my beak in it.

Looking through recipes—Here's a cake I'll make. (It was a pickle recipe.)

Please hurry and tie my shoes—but don't rush. We have a football but not a full grown one.

I dreamed it was Christmas and everyone got presents but me.

Are these war beans? (Navy beans) This is the backest, Mom. (furtherest back)

We can't go see her 'cause we don't know what her house looks like.

How come you never told me this before. (We were talking about hospital costs to get him.)

Who is president? But I thought you said John Paris was elected. (US and school board.)

I told Wayne he was put in an incubator in the hospital right after his birth.) An incubator! Did they think I was a chicken egg???!!

THE LAST CATTLE DRIVE

On an early crisp fall afternoon excitement filled the air. My husband and I strolled over to join some spectators watching the distant dust trail to come closer. It was some time before the cattle herd and horseback cowboys appeared in view.

The last big cattle drive of the era was approaching it's destiny. Cattle drivers had been on the trail several days and were pushing the last several miles to reach Crawford. Cattle owner, Jim Daniels of Buffalo Gap, South Dakota, (originally from across the road from the Gibbons farm/ranch) brought his herd of cattle on the trail 80 miles, crossing several creeks, for dispersion in the Crawford Livestock Market.

Harold and I were more than casual spectators, our young sons were riding into the corrals in the old chuck wagon with their friend and the wagon master the last miles. This was like in olden days—an unusual opportunity in 1968.

"This reminds me," began our companion, 90 year old Joe Sikorski, "of the last cattle drive I saw go through here from Texas." It had taken place 70 years earlier. The weathered cowboy, still at ease on his horse, spoke of the herd, several hundred long horned cattle and the cowboys driving north along the dusty trail from Texas to South Dakota.

"I was several miles west of Crawford, by the Downey place," Mr. Sikorski continued. "I had a homestead cabin there and had gone to Crawford for groceries. It was a Saturday night and I was on my way home. I drove my team and wagon over the crest of a big hill just before the draw when I noticed their campfire. The drovers had settled their herd and, except for a lone watchman, were spread out resting for the night. The watchman rode over and quietly asked me not to go near their herd.

"Any stampede of that many cattle would be impossible to stop. I rode slowly around and after that I always went way around that draw to go to town. The drovers camped there for a week or more before moving on. There was plenty of good grass in that valley. The cattle were being driven to the Pine Ridge Indian

Reservation in South Dakota for the Sioux Indians. The herd was sent by our government to give the Indians stock cattle so they could raise their own herd. The Indians used these cattle for food. I heard they butchered and ate all of that herd of beef during that winter.

"After the cattle were moved on to South Dakota I saw the remains of several cow carcasses. The cowboys driving the cattle ate good on beef rations too," Mr. Sikorski said.

Mr. Sikorski came to Dawes County from Germany in 1888. He said he had watched cattle drives from Texas before, when herds numbered in the thousands and the valley was covered with long horned cattle. He saw other herds going to the Reservation. He said the government hired men to show these people how to plant potatoes to raise their own food. Government men plowed a furrow and demonstrated dropping potatoes in the ground every few steps. Watching carefully the Indians returned under cover of night and dug up every potato. They ate all the potatoes before any could grow, Mr. Sikorski said.

Noise of the cattle brought our visit to a halt. The dust and smells of the herd was close at hand. The cattle had reached their destination. We watched Mr. Sikorski stroll off in his well worn high heeled cowboy boots and sweat stained, black felt hat, before picking up our own young cowboys for their trip back to country school. Our sons were a part of history which we talked about on the trip back to school. We would long remember this cattle drive experience.

OUR PONY

In the 1970s, my family and I enjoyed attending the Fort Robinson Art show. I greatly admired the art work by some outstanding artists. My favorite was Hildred Goodwine, an Arizona lady who painted realistic horses and children. She was talented in her paintings of subjects appreciated by our interest—horses and children.

I commented to my family on the superb art quality at the art show. We had ideas about the outstanding art we liked. We agreed that a most admired was the horse paintings by Mrs. Goodwine. If I had money to purchase a painting, I would have selected the horse head she displayed framed in her booth. Mrs. Goodwine was a sweet lady who took time to show my small daughter how to draw horses.

We were surprised, when a short time later, a letter came stating we would receive a package of a horse picture in the mail. When the box arrived, we found a large wooden frame box nailed shut. Inside was a glass covered framed picture of a horse head done in chalk on velvet. The drawing was of our pony! I had shared a snap shot of our pony and little daughter with Peggy who years before lived near by and dated my father-in-law. The picture was an impressively well done chalk drawing by a young friend of hers. The gift showed artistic talent of Cammy Crabtree and Peggy, who at past 75 years, nailed the crate together herself to mail that horse picture. Cammy did the chalk drawing in art class. We were excited as we carefully pulled nails to see the picture inside the package before their dad came in from the hayfield. The picture was large and and beautiful. We appreciated it even more than the famous artist's picture because this picture was of our favorite pony.

Our little ones excitedly showed their Dad the picture of Prince pony. Their Dad was impressed with the drawing, "That looks just like Prince," he said. Prince was a family favorite on the place for years. My children to rode him to school, to round up cattle and they let the neighbor children ride him. They taught their children to ride on Prince. We have photographs of little grandsons riding Prince. I rode Prince to move cattle and to round up cattle.

Recently Peggy's daughter wrote, then called to to say she saw a story I had written. She enclosed a picture of Gramps with his Maxwell car, which on the back her mother had written, "Send this to the Gibbons family someday." It was a joyful reunion and exchange with some special people and reminisces. I have a copy of the photo I took and an original chalk drawing of our pony plus memories of a friend who befriended our little girl. This was an example of rural people, the culture of western ways. Our good friends and Prince the pony will long be remembered.

Beth with grandchildren, Will, Mindy, Ben, Ana, Andy holding greats Joey and Addie, Alyssa, Ashley, Marina, Jade , Ivan and Cody in front holding great grandson Carson, in 2009.

BLESSINGS

Blessings can, and often do, come in small packages. I recently spent the a day with my son and family. His oldest son brought over their new baby to show. What a thrill to hold a ten day old baby. He is perfect in every way and so good. The proud father was happy to have his grandma hold and love this precious baby boy.

Our senses are a wonderful blessing to posses. Ask anyone who has lost any of their senses. You will get an idea of how important they are. Most of us can see, feel, taste and hear. Our senses may not be as sharp as they once were but we still have much to be grateful for. The gift of loving and being loved is worth giving thanks.

Other blessings I have been thinking about include blessings of health, homes, and family. A place to lay our heads at night reminds me of our soldiers, including my nephews and my grandson. There are no comforts of home and family in Iraq and Afghanistan.

Remembering my parents and grandparents brings a grateful appreciation for the up bringing they gave us. Our mother stayed home, took care of the family, did cooking and housework while our father took responsibility to earn a living and helping with the family. They were involved in our lives. We did our share to help. What needed done, we did when we could.

The older I get the more I realize how wise our family is and was. We had grandparents close by to visit and enjoy time together. Our parents and grandparents were concerned for their children and grandchildren. Family time is worth working for. Grandparents have a sense of time that is unlike parents who have work to accomplish every day. I am grateful to be able to share time with my grandchildren.

Our parents were not lax on disciplining. We caught it for misbehavior. We accepted their counsel and tried to do better next time. They encouraged us to be the best we could—we tried. We went to school to learn and were grateful to teachers who helped. When we were in trouble at school we heard about it at home. Our mother and father listened and encouraged.

Littlest granddaughter made plans to decorate for Thanksgiving. She is enthusiastically involved. We write what each is thankful for. Old traditions and new will include a table cloth made by my mother and a roaster used by my mother-in-law for years. Dishes are old but we enjoy them. Recipes may be tried and true but some will be new. She can set the table and feel a kinship to her heritage. Like the pilgrims of old, I am thankful for the freedoms to worship and to thank God for times with family and an ever grateful heart.

HONESTY

Sometimes it is better to laugh than cry about a situation. I had such a moment when a cowboy invited me to 'dinner.' I was thinking of the invitation as a friendship so I replied, "Okay, I'll eat with you." Then he quickly added he needed to know the age of anyone he dated. The dating idea was a surprise to me and a different kind of meal proposal than I have ever encountered.

Being the honest person I am, I told the age I would be the following month. My mother taught us that telling the truth is best. He gasped, admitting that he thought I was years younger. Just because he is younger, he assumed I was. I believe he was the looser. I never heard from that 'young man' again. I eventually told my grown children the story. We enjoyed a good laugh. We laughed over the story again later when they shared with their families. I am just getting brave enough to share the story with others.

My pen pal, Eileen in Illinois, with whom I have corresponded with for as many years as that young man has been around, was next. She enjoyed the incident and laughed more than most. Eileen and I have shared stories through letters for many years. This incident was a topper. She was still laughing heartedly when I said, "Good bye" and hung up the phone.

Since I shared 'the dinner invitation story' with a few friends. Some said, "I will take you to dinner and I won't even ask your age!" That turned the incident into a winner.

COUNTRY SIT-COM

Years ago a friend with children near the age of ours said, "Your life is more exciting than a television sit-com. You should write a book!" I have pondered her thoughts through the years. I'm beginning to believe she was right. Living in the country doesn't sound exciting but there is always something happening around this place.

The 'happening' that day was a laying hen that fell into a feeder and couldn't get out. Linda was aware of a milk cow chasing me shortly before our first born arrived. I was so scared I just stood still yelling. My beloved husband came running, waving a large stick and loudly shouting at the cow. The cow suddenly stopped. I didn't trust her after that. She got wrong side up in a canyon several years later. I didn't feel as sorry as I might have. She was a mean cow.

My husband rushed in the house breathless one windy summer night yelling, "Grab a flashlight!" as he reached for his sixteen gage shotgun and shells. We cautiously walked outside to where the wind whistled. He shot and decapitated a rattle snake coiled by the brooder house door. "Rattle snakes usually travel in pairs," he said, as he turned, shining the flashlight by the brooder house. I caught my breath, for coming around the corner was another rattle snake slithering toward the brooder house door and us. I had been outside shutting that door for our baby chicks just a few minutes earlier—bare footed. This was my first encounter with rattle snakes! The next snake I saw by the house was a harmless little garter snake. I didn't take time to check for rattlers. I destroyed that poor garter snake and the hoe handle without taking time to look at the tail to see if it was a poisonous rattler.

A pig eating chickens was another subject of conversation. I ran for my husband in the field weeks before our first baby was born. He said he feared I was starting labor. I was to get him if it was time to go to the hospital, half an hour away. A hen was under attack by a sow and I was determined to stop her. Dear husband was an understanding animal lover.

Baby kittens found hidden were exciting events for young family members and for me. Our little boys came running excitedly telling me about this funny grunting noise they heard in a hay stack by the barn. In their arms were half a dozen brown fuzzy baby puppies—'the grunting noises.' Our happy boys found the new baby puppies.

A litter of puppies were born in the garage when it was below zero outside were brought in to warm with my hair dryer, heat lamp and a lot of rubbing. Most survived by gentle caring hands of family members working for hours. Eric, who became a 4-H show dog was one of the rescued puppies. Other times it was baby pigs, calves or kittens we warmed and revived with time and effort.

Daily, cattle or pigs get out of their pasture and pens. They must be chased in. One early morning I took a quick run to the Sudan field to chase out several ornery determined cows. Our dog was in the adjoining pasture close by, frolicking with a coyote! The next morning I took along the 22 rifle. I didn't see the coyote again though I continued to carry the rifle. Country people need and use ammunition to defend their lives and their property.

I have a picture taken by our young son of a young weaner pig robbing our milk cow. It took awhile to solve that mystery. Our oldest was the first to spot and photograph the villain.

A good sized bucket calf turned on the barn lights with his tongue. Hubby finally found him in action reaching his tongue to the switch nearby. Harold solved that problem by nailing up a board over the switches. We had wondered why a light was on and our electric bill was rising.

Our family dog was bitten by a rattle snake—twice. The first time she was defending our yard from a slithering, rattle snake sliding under the fence toward the garden. The snake bit Pepsi dog on the tongue as she shook it. Pepsi survived due to the quick thinking of our sons. A polis quickly applied to her tongue drew out the poison. We continued giving her extra loving care, soft food and lots of fresh water, as she nursed her baby puppies. Later she attacked an extremely large rattle snake hidden in a soap weed in the hills to defend her master who rushed for a long stick to get the snake. The fastest I ever saw him drive was when we took our furry family protector to the veterinarian. The bite, in her neck, sadly proved agonizingly painful and fatal.

Little son ran to tell me he spotted a small snake by the house. I ran outside following him. He pointed to a huge colorful yellow cabbage worm. Younger son's report of a snake behind the porch door was real, a good sized coiled prairie rattler. I quickly got the garden hoe and took care of that snake. A tiny snake in the wood box in the porch was also a real rattlesnake. Cows bit by rattlesnakes were doctored and watched carefully.

We pulled porcupine needles from our dogs, cows and horses. Gloves, pliers and extra hands to hold the hurting animals was the way we handled them. The worst most painful needles were inbedded inside the roof of the dogs' mouth or in their nose. Animals knew we were helping but those needles hurt. A horse we tried got porcupine quills in his nose.

Riding calves or cows was fun for our sons. They proved they were cowboys by holding ropes and helping with livestock work. Country living has intriguing moments. I have shot wild varmints out of tree tops; I hit three raccoon with four 22 shells high on an electric pole after they were in our garden corn. Our dogs bark until we captured or disposed of offending critters.

Cows were bawling at the corral gate lately. I let them to the tank but that was not what they wanted. I decided it must be coyotes or a bobcat bothering them making them uneasy or maybe flies.

My older son ran rushing into the kitchen so out of breath I couldn't understand his words. Our truck had caught fire in the wheat field and he was trying to say, "Call the fire department." I couldn't make sense of his words. The truck burned up quickly but the family survived. We were thankful for our efficient volunteer fire department. Our daughter-in-law was in the truck with her preschool nephew. Thankfully, all were fine and the fire was quickly extinguished. We were grateful, a flaming fire could have been much worse. No time for more rural life stories because it's time to check on the animals.

WILDFIRE

Our family survived a week of intense heat surrounded by out of control wildfires during the summer of 2006. Plans for the week were changed really fast!

Numerous people were evacuated from homes, nursing homes and hospitals. The thought of multiple fires out of control, caused by lightening burning around us, jumping from pine tree to tree, is nerve wrecking. The electricity was off caused by burned poles. Some ranchers lost thousands of acres of grass and hay land. Thick smoke causes headaches and severe sinus problems for many.

Several of my family members were here for more than a few nights. That is with their multiple vehicles, animals, horses, dogs and cats. They borrowed a horse trailer to get horses loaded and moved here to be safe quickly. Horses offered no resistance to loading as the thick dark smoke was threatening. Beds were made up and filled all over my house. We had a good time as a family despite nervous concerns. Littlest granddaughter kept the rest involved with kittens and 'Norby,' a grown cat she especially liked. Baby kittens had plenty of attention when she was near.

The telephone continued ringing with friends and neighbors from near and far checking to see if our family was alright. I appreciated the genuine show of concern. Several called repeatedly day after day. Many letters were written containing questions and concerns.

The smoke drifted in heavy and billowed high in the sky to the west and to the east of us. One morning we could not see the nearby big butte because of the intense dark smoke. My brother-in-law developed dust pneumonia from the smoke. Our family was among the many listed for evacuation though no one came knocking on my door. Fires were several miles from here in all directions. I didn't move out because I was needed here for my family.

My son and compassionate daughter-in-law were extremely concerned about their army son's car and their living room full of the couple's wedding gifts. The parents carefully loaded the car and drove it to a shed where it stayed for years until they returned from military duty.

The sun went down in a blaze of brilliant red across the western sky. It was still bright red the next morning when we could see it through the smoky haze. Since the smoky fog has finally lifted and our lives drifted back to some semblance of normal. My family and I were extremely thankful that the fires did not get any closer and no lives were lost.

FIRST TRACTOR
Harold G as told to Beth

"My Dad was a horse farmer. He said it took a day to plow one acre with an old walking plow. Then he plowed with horse drawn plows with seats to ride. He plowed many acres that way. I remember feeling disappointed every time he brought home another team of horses. I wanted him to buy a tractor. Horses were 'reluctant farmers' and they died easily.

"In December 1940, the local John Deere dealer, Jim Soester, brought out a little John Deere H and a two bottom plow to demonstrate on our place. He drove it a short distance then asked me to drive it. I drove several rounds while the dealer took pictures. My picture, driving that tractor, was up in his office for several years after that.

"Jim Soester measured and said we were plowing a good ten inch furrow. I was impressed and I liked the tractor. The following spring Dad finally bought a brand new John Deere H which cost $680. We used it for all our field work and for grinding feed. Dad had me do most of the farming from then on—I was 16 years old.

"The John Deere H seems like a toy now but that little tractor did a lot of work. I drove it to pull a horse binder. Day after day, I cut wheat and oats with that tractor. It took a lot of days to grind out a field but the job was completed with less stress than with horses. It was a big improvement in farming.

"My Dad drove the tractor while I rode a one row horse lister. The John Deere H was adaptable to use with a lot of horse machinery. I would get off at the end of each row to pull the pin to adjust the rows correctly.

"I drove the John Deere H to cultivate corn with the horse cultivator. The horse mower worked fine behind the H too. It seemed a big advancement over the hay burning horses we had always used. Horses disliked going over the same ground again and again. The little H, Johnny Putt, would go right along without coaxing.

"We sold the H after several years of use to the local sale barn for $700. The little H had earned my respect. I now have newer John Deere tractors for my field work. Each tractor I own can do more than the previous models.

"I have been a John Deere fan since that December day in 1940. I still admire the little two cylinder H and have fond memories it generated. I hope to get enough parts to restore an 'H' to running conditions. My sons and grandsons will cheer for me and the little John Deere H when I do."

Dad with eight of his great grandchildren celebrating his 87th Birthday at Fort Robinson, in 1985. Ashley and Tyler didn't know Great Grandpa's are shared!

GRANDCHILDREN

A grandmother's greatest joy is love and affection from her grandchildren. They share our heritage and look up like she is the smartest person. They give their best drawings for hanging on the refrigerator. They offer candy, hugs and sticky kisses. They devote efforts to fill the world with action. I remember the first time I held each one.

Andy was fair, quiet and special. He looked very tiny in the hospital. He reminded me of his father and grandfather and he wanted to be like his Grandpa. He went along whenever he could to haul ground corn for pigs. Andy and Will scooped feed off the pickup with a tiny shovel. They really liked to help their Grandpa and Grandma.

Willy had lots of dark hair standing straight as a precious bundle of all boy. He was a brave little guy who preferred to ride Jess, the biggest horse. He was a serious fun grandson who hated turkeys but cautiously touched them when I held them.

Joey was fair and quiet and interested in many things with plans to teach. He enjoyed feeding our calf called Baby. He collected colored feathers from our chickens, ducks and turkeys at each visit to the farm. Feathers always remind me of Joe.

Cody was a dark eyed delight. He was bright and active at holiday time, he showed his original costume each year and shared whatever he had. He liked riding sawhorses and real horses. Cody was happy in the country participating in various 4-H projects.

Grandsons played with Baby, the orphan calf, and took turns feeding him from a big bottle, even after he grew big. Baby, the bottle fed calf, grew so huge he frightened me.

Ashley, my first granddaughter was beautiful, blond and loved spending time with me. I needed her comfort. She had big blue eyes and a beautiful smile. Her mother said I could take her to Sunday School and church the summer of 92. She was a blessing to hug and hold.

Little Mindy said, "I love you Grandma," clearly, though she was from Romania, on the first a phone call. She named all her dolls and knew who gave each. She is an active dark eyed beauty, so rhythmical and musically inclined, she amazes me.

Ana came shyly running to her Daddy in Romania and stood quietly while I took their picture. She had fun trying on clothes, brought for her. She thought she was in America in a bare upstairs apartment as she had a Daddy, Grandma and a suitcase full of pretty things.

Alyssa was a miniature doll arriving 9-11-03 and weighing five pounds one ounce. At three she calls to ask, "Are you coming to church Grandma?" Or, "The dress fits perfectly." She wore an old dress that belonged to her great grandmother for a picture.

Ivan, from Russia, exuberantly ran hard to greet me for a hug knocking me down. He asked many questions and remains interested in everything, especially things mechanical. Ivan said, "I love my parents" then asked, "Why did it take them so long to find me?"

Ben, of Russia, is a cherub with fat rosy cheeks and a bold way of striding though he is small. He was afraid of nurses; they hurt him changing bandages and putting in IVs. He is a bright beautiful boy with a mischievous grin. He talks clearly and loves to play on computer.

Marina, of Ukraine, is beautiful and appreciative of attention. She laughs at my mistakes on the phone and says, "I love you Grandma" and "Oh, Grandma!" when I ask dumb questions.

Jade of China, is a sweet bright little girl. She stays close to me with big smiles and hugs. "I want to sit beside you," she says when I am with the family. She has many questions.

Great grandchildren are a bonus. Four little great great grandchildren Carson, Joey, Addie and Baby Treye make me feel loved when they run to greet me. The newest is too tiny to walk yet but he will in a year's time. I love them dearly. Grandchildren are a special delight for the happiness and joy shared.

WRITING JOYS

Some times it pays to do what you know you should. I bought a magazine, because I felt I should, as I had been looking at it while waiting for my tire repair. I never dreamed the route I was headed. Because the magazine was expensive, I decided to ask about writing for them. I could write about rural Nebraska living.

The magazine was mostly about ranches in Arizona and Nevada and they needed to expand their horizons to Nebraska was my thought. I decided to contribute so I sent an article I had written a short time earlier.

My first piece, accepted! I received extra copies of the magazine and a good sized check. I was pleased so I sent another story. This time I included pictures to accompany the article. This too was accepted with a bigger check and extra copies for my family.

I was surprised when I received a telephone call one evening from a former Nebraskan living in California. He had, at one time, lived in the Sandhills near Stapleton where the sod house picture in the story was taken. He later sent me his writings about military life and has called occasionally. He sent me a copy of a book he wrote. I have a new friend.

Another former Nebraskan from North Carolina wrote and sent a copy of his book about living in the Nebraska Sandhills northeast of where I grew up. It was interesting reading and I wrote to thank him telling how I appreciated his book. Next he sent a copy of the Christian School material that he edits. I found this magazine is impressive and worthwhile reading to share with family and friends. Another new friend via e-mail.

Todays mail brought a letter from a lady in rural Idaho. She too saw an article in the same magazine and wanted to re-connect with the Gibbons as her mother had years before. Her mother was a former western Nebraska lady who wrote to me and my young daughter. The real surprise clincher was a picture on which her mother had written on the back requesting, "Return to the Gibbons family someday." The picture is my father-in-law standing beside his new 1918 Maxwell car. The car was donated to the scrap drive during the war in early 1940s. I never saw it so felt this was a thoughtful gesture and much appreciated by my family. Her mother had written, "I get to ride in this." She called the car a "Joy Buggy." This picture and note impressed my family. They had heard about the Maxwell through the years.

Writing fever is fun. I am glad I embarked on this trail. Meeting people through the mail from all over makes the road more worthwhile. We don't know what is waiting beyond the next publication. Words have power to encourage, connect and bring peace. I think we are all empowered to use our God given talents to help others. You never know where they might lead or who you will meet through your efforts.

WARMING SOLUTION

My hair dryer was the handiest tool for warming and drying young livestock in extreme cold weather. I loved using the dryer to save baby animals. I rarely used it for me. I don't have time to sit around with a dryer.

We used that hairdryer on baby calves when they were found chilled and shivering. They were carried into the kitchen from outside on cold mornings. Then the family would get busy rubbing towels or rags. We took turns holding the dryer on coldest places— little ears, feet and legs. It may take hours but it works; it was a life saver for the stock man's herd.

Baby kittens were revived though they were thoroughly soaked in a spring rain. We thought they were drowned but the hair dryer warmed them so they were soon fuzzy and purring. What a delight for curious young country children.

The hair dryer was used to revive litters of new born pigs. It didn't take long for them to begin wiggling and squealing for food. We massaged their little bodies and worked with them until they were on their feet. One January we discovered a litter of baby puppies in the garage. It was below zero when they were discovered—some were stiff from the cold. We all, dad, mother, sons and little sister, worked with puppies until they were stretching and yawning with innocence. Aric, a little brown puppy we revived, went on to become a 4-H trophy winner for his mistress at the county fair. She was proud of showing him.

Aric, as a grown dog remained a faithful family pet years later staying under the pickup after his master's fatal heart attack. He waited grieving for days. Aric died a short time later. I think our dog died of a broken heart. Farmer and Aric were loyal companions riding in the pickup to check the cattle every day for years. Aric liked being involved with Farmer and his family. He kept the cattle back when mother or young ones were inside the cab. Aric was a great guard dog as well as a good show dog obeying commands.

That hair dryer is a modern wonder for farm women and men who need a warm wand to revive chilled baby livestock. I highly recommend a hair dryer.

CONTESTS

Challenges can be fun. I entered poetry contests and received notices that my poems are in books with certificates of accomplishment and offers to sell them. I didn't buy. I really wonder if they write the same to every entrant. Poetry is a fun way to express thoughts in a concise clear form. I write about activities in years past, ancestors, Sandhills and country life and features of interesting people. These topics are close to my heart. I like writing but I refuse to pay for the privilege. This year I won the state home extension poetry contest and a check.

Several years ago I took a class called "Sandhills Journey." Poetry seemed an ideal way to reflect in writing about the country where I grew up. Concrete evidence on paper was to show the importance of Sandhills to my fellow teachers and students as examples.

My poem 'Sandhills Sunshine', seemed inspired. I printed it on a green poster board with Sandhill pictures and laminated for the 'Sandhills Journey' project. This is a way to relate and to think about what is important. Teachers, from far away learned about the Sandhills and some thought they were at the end of the world. I laughed, as I met friends wherever we went.

I entered a recipe contest to share a recipe and story of its origin. The prize was a free cook book. This contest was exciting to win and more so when I learned that my daughter's recipe also won a cook book. Our recipes are pictured along with 132 winners. Winning those cookbooks felt good and more so when we learned there were hundreds of entries.

Writing contests can be fun. I continue entering contests as a challenge. They make me determined to do what I enjoy and to improve. I think about Waldo McBurney, a bee producer of Quinter, Kansas, who entered walking competitions after he was older. He kept entering after he was 100. He wrote, "There aren't as many competitors when you get in the old age bracket." McBurney wrote a book, 'My First 100 Years, a Look Back From the Finish line' in 2004 when he was 104 years old. He shared his faith, family history and about the fun of walking. "This will probably be my only book," he wrote. My son, Wayne bought the book directly from the author, at 106, and was impressed to meet such an inspiring character. He was at that time still walking about a mile daily to the post office for his mail.

Years back I was in a beauty contest with Teddi, Angel and Katherine. We were instructed to line up and smile for the judge. We quietly obeyed and waited for the judges decision. A few minutes later the verdict was announced. "And the winner is," pause for emphasis, "Teddi Bear!" The contest was set up by my four year old daughter after she had watched Miss American contest on television the day before. She was impressed and wanted her own beauty contest. I lost in a beauty pageant to a well worn stuffed brown teddy bear! That was the only beauty contest I ever entered. My little girl and I had fun and the contest made interesting conversation. The judge's father and brothers laughed.

IMPORTANT

What is important?
Big shiny cars, late nights,
What makes life right?

How do we bequeath love?
Teenage sons drove a rattly car
On a trip to join family afar.

Sons taught many that day
A boot sole began to show wear
Duck tape mended the tear.

They didn't panic or hesitate.
Their presence was quietly felt
Great uncle's farewell dealt.

I'm proud they're my sons
Their tribute will survive
From college, a long drive.

A trip worthwhile to recall
Duck tape, a very old car
Fond memories of a trip afar.

We laugh to recall the day

Sons made a presence known
Love of great uncle was shown

TRIBUTES

PARENT TRIBUTE

Our parents organized Sunday School and invited teachers and board members to meet in our home. Mom kept school census records for as long as I can remember. Mom and Dad invited visiting ministers to stay in our home with limited space. We had no running water, telephone or electricity and only a privy standing at the end of a path. We lived two hours from any town on trail roads.

There was no women's fellowship until our Mama began one. She invited neighbors in. One brought boxes of overalls to patch so they patched overalls. Mama said she preferred fancy work for a change. She embroidered and tied quilts while we children 'helped' beneath the frame. Mama and Dad were decisive in organizing workers. When friend/neighbor, Ida Flowerdew, had a baby, Mom helped 4-H youth embroidery a baby quilt. She put the blocks together and we delivered a lovely hand stitched quilt to a grateful happy couple.

Activities, education and Christian enrichment functioned because of our Mom and Dad. They worked side by side to milk cows, repair and garden. They provided enthusiasm and incentives to succeed. They read books to us at night and on cold days while snow shifted and blew. Mom read a scripture calendar encouraging us to memorize.

My button collection was my mom's idea. Buttons were sewn on cloth salt sack pages. Friends and relatives contributed pretty and unusual buttons. Some came from old wedding dresses. Neighbors brought buttons to school. Hosts at 4-H meetings often got out their button jars. There are/were hundreds of buttons sewed in my old button book.

Our mom sewed doll clothes for my dolls when I was to recite a piece to them for a Christmas program. When it was program time, lanterns were lit and hung from ceiling hooks. I felt like I had the best part with my dolls in new clothes. This was a gift of time from my mama who did all the cooking, sewing, and preserving from their large garden. New dresses were of feed sack material made by our mother or hand downs sometimes redesigned. Mom taught herself, and me, to crochet. She and Dad shared pictures and told stories of family. Meeting relatives from miles away was fun—we recognized them through family stories and pictures.

A teacher failed to show up so our mom taught us a number of days or weeks. She held classes until the teacher returned. A boy confided, "Irene taught the first lesson I had all year."

Mom attended college to get re-certified in 1943, when there was no teacher. Dad did extra work and took on full children responsibilities. Mom sewed burlap sack curtains our school stage. They organized our 4-H club. Youth for miles around joined. We had a fund raiser, built a hall for exhibits and held the '4-H Tri-County Fair.' Mom bought ribbon and made prizes with us helping. They contacted George B. German who interviewed youth on his radio program about 4-H projects. I was chosen by Mr. German to tell about my forestry book.

There was no Daily Vacation Bible School so Mom drove our pickup and took us six, gathering many neighbors along the way. We rode sitting in the back as she drove an hour on trail roads to Bible School for a week at Elsmere. She repeated the trail delivering everyone home again. She helped at Bible School with extra work. Our parents didn't discuss problems; they were innovative and we grew up learning to help.

Thank you notes were part of gift receiving. We wrote a letter immediately after opening gifts. Mom and Dad said letter writing was important and we wrote. Years later my aunt sent me a thank you letter I had written to her at age six.

When we began leaving home Mom wrote, sharing activities and family news. The folks didn't ask anyone to do a job they weren't willing to do. They taught by working side by side on tasks. When we were asked to do a job it was done with respect to them. They were leaders and a positive influence. Thanks to our parents support the community thrived. They set standards to do what was right. 'Always do your best' was a motto our mom repeated. Our parents caring shaped our lives. They continue to influence our thinking.

VETERANS DAY
By Joe Gibbons 1988-1999

Flags today in tribute wave,
for those loyal ones who gave
of their youth, their hopes, their might,
For a cause they knew was right.

Morning bells sound their call,
Pause and say a prayer for all,
All who served valiantly,
That men might be ever free.

Toll bell, drums slow beat,
Silence falls in every street.
In each heart swells the plea,
Keep us safe, but keep us free.

VETERANS

In1995 I wrote a story that made front page in The Chadron Record, with a big headline and several pictures. This is a favorite story of the many published stories that I have written. The story and side stories were researched of the invasion and battle on Iwo Jima 50 years before. I wrote and called many who shared names of family or friends who knew more soldiers. I included pictures of Marines in uniform, who put their lives on the line, February 19, 1945. Local soldiers of all branches of military bravely served. Each one I called referred me to another. I located seven Marines in Dawes County who were in the service on Iwo Jima. They were unaware their neighbors were Marines in the same battle.

I called my Uncle Chester Weber in Lincoln, who served on the battleship Yorktown as a radar man and wrote in his diary every day. I asked questions of a local attorney who was on the same ship of several thousand working below. They served off the shore of Iwo Jima.

When I invited the local Marines to meet for lunch, they were hesitant—but they came! Several wives, my sister included, said they had never heard so much talk of the difficult days in Iwo Jima. Some brought souvenirs, others listened and quietly shared with a few. I heard of the wild hogs they roasted, of horrible smells and sounds and hiding in caves throughout the tiny triangle shaped island. It was, I hope and pray, healing for them and for their wives. I felt good to be involved. I was thankful I had arranged a meeting of our local heroes.

Later I wrote to our state capital asking if these Iwo Jima veterans could be honored as "Admirals in Nebraska's Navy." We met again and this time, I was humbled and honored to distribute certificates recognizing every one of 'my soldiers' as Nebraska Navy Admirals. They deserved the recognition and I think they were pleased.

While substitute teaching later, an assignment was for students to read aloud, The Code Talkers, an impressive story of radio men in Iwo Jima. Several students were continually interrupting, disturbing the class with laugher and loud talking. I stopped the reading and told them of an elderly man north of Crawford who was a Sea bee in Iwo Jima and of other US Marines living nearby. That night I copied the Iwo Jima news story and pasted it on a large poster board for the teacher to laminate and share with students. I included several photographs of the Iwo Jima veterans meeting in our town. Next time the teacher can prepare her students by explaining that these local men were involved in that most horrific battle and survived. Many of their comrades and close friends did not!

We need to be aware of the price of freedom! We should never forget our brave military forces. It has been 65 years since the battle of Iwo Jima. We must remember them and their bravery. I will continue to write about military heroes whenever I can.

IWO JIMA VETERAN

Most military veterans do not discuss their experiences, especially when they were so horrific it gives them nightmares. Anesthetic brings back fighting visions for some. They are thankful to have served and be safely back home among friends and family.

Johnny Ahrens, my brother-in-law, volunteered for the US Marine Corps, as a 17 year old, and was was sent to California then Hawaii and on to Iwo Jima. It was many years later that I talked to him about his experiences. I am extremely frustrated to see that new school text books devote only about three lines to the battle of Iwo Jima.

After several weeks of rigorous book camp training in California, the Marines were loaded for more training. John used vivid word pictures to describe his experiences. He was in Honolulu though he saw very little of the island. Enlisted men were confined to their quarters. He often said, "I have no desire to revisit those places, even in Hawaii."

It wasn't long before the Marines were considered combat ready. They were shipped overseas 'on a three month boat ride.' Food rations were limited to what they could could carry on their back. "It was beans and pork day after day," John said. "We were the fifth wave to land on Iwo Jima. Multitudes of fatalities were under foot. The gate lowered and we plunged into neck deep cold water holding our guns and ammunition above our heads. The other side of the island was covered with mine traps," he said.

The Marines moved forward keeping a sharp eye out for hidden dangers. Johnny said, "One Jap managed to hide under a pile of bodies and was sniping at our men." He caught the lead when he was located. John remembered going out on patrol many nights with three men and only one or two returned. Friends were permanently separated by a rifle shot under cover of darkness. Suicide dive bombers, kamikaze, were a constant threat. A bullet grazed Johnny's head just above the left ear, while he was on the battle line, he lost a strip of hair. Officers saw the blood and told him to report to the purple heart booth to collect his medal. He said he got in line where saw so many soldiers in worse condition than he and became upset. He decided to go back and take out his frustrations on the enemy.

Bombs were dropped and the war was over. The Marines were taken to Japan where they walked through total destruction. Nothing but a rare fraction of a building frame stood. John said he never wanted to see anything like that again. The sights and stench were awful. Japanese were stripped and shoved through disinfecting tanks as they were corralled as prisoners of war. It was dehumanizing for enemy and soldiers, Johnny reported.

War experiences influenced lives of men who returned home. They sincerely hope and pray war will never be repeated for any generation. Johnny was very thankful to be an ex-Marine. His brothers Rudolph, Pete and Junior all served in the army. Johnny appreciated country life and worked as a self employed trucker then as a farmer and a combiner.

Johnny married my sister, Lila on April 15, 1955 in Chadron with friends, Ralph Wohlers and Almetta Wallace for attendants. They have three grown sons: Lee John, Tom Dale and Joe David; grandchildren, Kim, Ben, Coleman, Ian and Logan and great grandson Tayten. Johnny died of cancer July 19, 2008, before getting to know his great grandsons. The family lived south of Chadron on the Table, on the Marcus Cain place, on Tom Muldoon farm then on his parent's place, the original Henry Ahrens farm where Lee and Cindy and Lila still live. Tom lives nearby and Joe and Paula are living near Palmer, Alaska.

WHY?

Brave young men going off to war
To foreign lands they've not heard of before
Their knees shake and their mothers cry
Some reporters keep asking, "Why?"

Brave young men from every walk of life
Make it through battles and enemy strife
Each day's a struggle to fight and not cry
Now many at home are asking, "Why?"

Soldiers brave, march on scorched land
They answer their country's demand
They fight for freedom and for family
They fight without an uttered, "Why?"

Soldiers fight as long as they can
Boys fight and quickly becomes a man
They know each day could be their last sigh
Still some continue asking "Why?"

Our country will eventually be free
As our brave young men fight for liberty
Freedom for you and for me, that's why!
Our Soldiers never question, "Why?"

Joe in wheel chair beside me, his Grandma Gibbons, holding his Eagle Quilt. The Eagle Pillow is behind his head.

LITTLE HERO

My youngest grandson Joey was a ten year old who liked time with family, friends and school. He had older brothers Andy and Willy and an adopted sister, Mindy. He was born July 19, 1988 in the Chadron Hospital, at 8 pounds and 8 ounces and was the pride of his family. He was a quiet sweet baby noticing everyone. He was baptized wearing a long white dress looking so precious the minister held him up for all to see. By fall Joey reached for brothers.

At eight months, Joey was crawling and cleaning out the toy box. He reached for Andy's birthday cake. Joey bruised easily but by nine months he was standing alone and crawling fast. "He smiles often," I wrote in a baby book. He walked by ten months and was cheerful, if he felt good. He was allergic to milk, wheat, oats, beans, dust, animal dander and smoke.

The Gibbons family traveled to Lincoln to meet Great Great Grandma Weber who was delighted and loved them and they her. Joey collected pretty feathers. He didn't like turkeys, they chased him. In the fall of 1991 a family picture was taken. Photographer asked for Grandpa and Grandma alone; Grandma asked to include grandsons. "Funny Grandma!," he said and little boys giggled. A picture of four little cousins holding baby puppies is 'our favorite.' Early May 1992 Joey, three, joined his brothers and cousin winning second prize competing in Crawford's turkey calling contest. Grandpa was very sorry he hadn't gone along to watch.

Baby bucket calf was fun. Bring out a bottle of milk and Baby, the calf, followed. Little boys called to inquire about Baby. They loved to feed him. Grandpa Harold suffered a fatal heart attack while checking his cows at noon May 18, 1992. The family quickly gathered to support and cry together. After the services, Joey, three, told Aunt Becky, "My Grandpa looks so nice, but he won't wake up." Prince Pony and Jess horse died the following summer. Little boys and I cried again; we miss their Grandpa and our horses.

Four grandsons stayed with Grandma for Bible School that summer. They enjoyed the day and evenings with Grandma. They slept together on a sofa bed. Joey was so grown up. Boys helped take baby kittens, chickens and ducks to show at Bible School. We talked about meeting Grandpas when we get to heaven. It was a bonding experience for them and me.

The Gibbons met in Ainsworth to attend a funeral for Great Grandma Weber on July 12, 1994. August 1996 brought a visit from Great Grandpa Weber and then shock at his very sudden heart attack. He is with our family in Heaven because he believes in Jesus too.

Joey sang in his Christmas program and looked so cute. He and best friend Matt are inseparable. Grandma, Dad and cousins climbed Gibbons hills to 'Bambi's Meadow.' Indian names, Old Woman and Little Princess are the ones I recall. A picnic lunch was fun. Joe earned presidential student athlete award in third grade as he wanted and found answers.

Laughter and games are good but Joey was sick. His mother took him to a doctor who declared he had the flu and sent him home. Next day, May 15, Joey was dizzy so his mother took him to a different doctor who ordered x-rays which showed a dark spot on his head. Joey was rushed on Flight for Life to Children's Hospital in Denver. Daddy in Cheyenne, rushed to meet the helicopter. Joey reported, "Dad was waiting when I got here." He held a Hug Bear tight. Doctors ran more tests. Joey continued to be brave though scared. He got sick inside the CAT scan. Doctor led his family to a dark windowless room and said the dark spot on Joey's brain stem was a stage four fatal tumor. He said they'd take out some of the tumor and do treatments. We prayed and cried. Joey told me, "Doctor will cut what he can and medicine will get the rest." Surgery took over three hours while we waited uneasily for a report.

Friends and family visited, others called. Joe was sedated with a turban bandage on his head. His parents and family took turns staying with him. A candy cart of treats came by each day. Joey asked his mother to get a candy bar for his stash to share. Joe requested black wind pants with snap sides and a black shirt like the Chicago Bulls for his trip home. He needed large ones to slip on. I took one picture in the hospital, at his mother's request, and Joey's displeasure. His mom thought he'd want to see what he looked like when he felt better. Joey never saw it, his eyes were weak and didn't focus clearly after surgery and treatments.

Make-A-Wish called asking Joe what he would like if he could have anything. He quietly replied, "Prayers." Asked where he'd like to go, he said "An African Safari." He wasn't up to that so they flew the family to Disney World. He spent most of his time sick in bed. He asked his dad, "Why are we parking in the handicapped spot? No one is handicapped in this car."

Grandma Beth hurried home to make an Eagle quilt for Joe, helped by special friend Jeanette Marshall. I'd promised, "A quilt for each grandchild." Joey liked his eagle quilt and matching pillow. I requested a picture of Grandma and Joey with his quilt. Later, he softly said, "Thank you for the quilt, I use it every day."

Joe learned to walk shuffling. He tried to keep up with school work. The family was informed the tumor had more than doubled and he had two weeks to live. His birthday was celebrated early. Joe greeted friends with joy. His hair was thin but his spirit was strong. Joe received messages from around the world; Internet connections sent prayers. A Sunday School class in Lincoln adopted Joe and wrote loving notes. A teacher in Australia had her class write and send coins. An Army family in Korea sent Korean money and pictures of Boeing planes and medals. Insignia and pictures came from Italy. Chicago Bulls sent bumper stickers and pens. Nebraska University and Chadron State invited Joe to football games. Brad Smith, Chadron State College coach, visited Joey and gave him a signed helmet asking him to be an honorary captain. He was honored but weak. The college president reported, "Joey should be our Most Valuable Player. He inspired the team to win." Nebraska University player, Eric Crouch sent Joe a signed picture which pleased him. Nebraska National Guard honored Joe in a hero ceremony October 17th. Alliance football team gave Joe a signed football and invited him to their game. Hemingford Bobcats recognized Joey with a red jersey, signed football and gloves. Joe was too sick to accept so big brother Andy stepped up for him.

Joe's faith was strong, he proclaimed, "I am healed of the Lord." He prayed for others and was an inspiration to all. Joey died October 31,1999, at 11 years. He wanted to be a teacher. His minister said, "Joe was a teacher. He reached his goal, teaching us to live with adversity and share a strong, positive faith." How can we do less? Joe's favorite Bible verse was Isaiah 40:31, "But they that wait upon the Lord shall renew their strength; they shall mount up with wings as eagles; they shall run and not be weary; and they shall walk and not faint."

RANCH/FARM TRIBUTE

In the wintertime, my Farmer/Rancher husband began his day by checking 'heavy' cows around 2 A.M. after checking them late before turning in. He may spend the night up watching cows. When they are okay he goes to bed to warm up for a few hours. He is up in time to see the horizon change from gray to shades of pink. He bundles up and takes a bucket of warm water to the chickens. He checks cows closely in the maternity shed and turns them to the stock tank. He carries heavy buckets of ground corn to feed a herd of hungry hogs. He expects a big breakfast when he comes inside.

Farmer eats breakfast of cooked cereal, milk and French toast with syrup and homemade butter then, it's time to put on heavy coveralls, big coat, warm cap, overshoes and mittens again. He tries to start a tractor to pull a hay stack. It won't start, it's too cold. He loads bales in the pickup and puts a couple sacks of cattle cake in the front. He drives to the herd where he throws out bales, or loose hay, drives ahead and throws out more hay over and over until it's unloaded. He cuts string on hay bales and scatters cattle cake for cattle until sacks are empty. He counts and checks cows and calves to be sure they are all okay.

Farmer gets his heavy ax and climbs down a steep bank to chop a hole in the creek for cattle to drink. In extreme cold the creek freezes nightly so cattle come running for water. He drives back to the yard and loads hay for another group of cattle. He unloads this and chops huge chunks of ice out of the tank. An ailing calf needs a penicillin shot and two bottles of warm milk replacer. It is fed three times a day for weeks. The herd of cows in the maternity shed are turned to feed and the tank then confined again.

It is past noon when Farmer comes to eat his noon meal, called dinner. Food has to be reheated by the time he is ready to sit at the table. Dinner is interrupted to run to the barn and chase a fence jumper cow back into the corral. It is bitter cold. The warmth of the wood stove inside makes a work weary Farmer sleepy. He half listens to as weather forecaster reports "The high for the day will be 20 degrees with a wind chill below zero."

"I'd better take a bottle of milk replacer when I go back," he says as he bundles up. I mix milk replacer, fill the bottle and hand it to him. He feeds the calf trying to get him on his feet and over to the mother cow. "Thought I might just as well stay out and feed while I was out," he confides hours later. He is too tired to talk as he eats a big bowl of homemade beef stew. He put a large chunk of wood in the stove and is asleep as soon as he hits the bed.

Calving cows are checked again during the night. Morning comes early, livestock must be looked after again. It is five degrees above so far. The landscape is covered with heavy frost and ground sparkles as the sun peeks through clouds.

It is past noon and time to bring bales to the last group of cattle. He chops the ice to break a hole and looks his animals over to be sure there isn't any with an ear down. Cold snow crunches and squeaks with each step as Farmer heads to the house. He stomps off excess snow and comes in bringing a burst of cold air. It's time to replenish his strength and prepare for more cold chores. He glances over the days mail and bundles up to go back out.

Time to take more milk to the calf then chop wood for the heater. We are all bundling up when—oops, the the phone rings. Someone saw our ad for firewood. They are on their way. We take milk to the calf, gather eggs and sort cattle for the night. Animals still need their feed and water. Wood buyers arrive and chores are stopped to help them load wood. Even that job is interrupted by a cow in labor. Farmer delivers the new calf and wipes it dry. He brings clean hay for their bed and alfalfa to feed the cow.

Daylight is past when the wood buyer drives down the road. Time to check cows in the far pen one more time before heading for the house. Farmer finds a new calf in a corner of the shed. It is chilled. Farmer carries the new calf to warmer quarters—our kitchen close to the warm wood burning stove. Farmer, sons and I begin vigorously rubbing calf using a heat lamp and my hair dryer. Later the baby calf finally stops shivering. Farmer tries to get calf to stand but it keeps falling. Finally some warm milk in her throat helps. It is still weak. Leftovers provide a simple supper. The calf in the kitchen is taken to the shed where it is put on clean hay beside his mother. It is past bedtime.

The next morning Farmer reports the calf we fed bottled powdered milk three times a day for weeks died in the night. The chilled calf is feeling frisky and doing fine. There are more baby calves requiring attention. Cows in the shed are monitored throughout the night and day. Baby pigs arrive on other cold nights. The winter routine continues.

Later when my Rancher/Farmer gets the flu and is too sick to work outside, it is me, his wife who takes over the responsibilities of the animal feeding routine. A piece of binder twine frozen in ice trips her. There is never a day without something happening. But the livestock must be fed and watered. Sons are in high school and hurrying to make it to school on time.

In spring it is time to plow and plant again. Machinery and tractors have to be oiled and checked carefully to be made ready for summer work. We may not feel like celebrating Ag Day. But, we are thankful for our health and strength to keep going.

We never cease to thrill at the arrival of each perfect new baby, be it calves, piglets, puppies, kittens, ducklings or chickens. Most exciting of all was our own three perfect babies. We are thankful for the privilege of living in the country and to raise our family here. The air is fresh and we are free to come and go as we choose and to raise our family with love. We can teach them responsibilities with the little animals they love to care for.

MY FARMER

In 1991-92, I wrote letters to my nieces' third grade class in Denver every month. I wanted to share life on the farm. I helped drive tractors and described work Farmer and I were doing. I told them about the changing jobs through seasons. I described machinery, John Deere tractors, animals-domestic and wild. I told them about the tame cows that ate cattle cubes from our hands. They were interested in Aric Dog who loved to ride with Farmer and went everywhere with him in the pickup. I told them about moving hay stacks to feed cattle in winter.

I wrote when we tied a calf and doctored it with a shot. We gathered eggs and packed them to sell. I told about ducks and turkeys followed grandsons and scared them. Also a bucket calf that followed me for his bottle of milk. Pigs aren't pretty but they grow fast. Cats followed as I walked the path to the mailbox every other day for mail.

These students were fascinated to learn about our horses and life in the country. Some wrote questions which I answered individually. One asked, "Do you live in a house or a cabin?" Another wrote about her horse. I was substitute teacher so I asked rural students to share their life with these city students. Each rural operation is unique. I asked if one girl would write to tell what a lariat is. She did and found a picture to help too.

Then came the most awful day of my life; my Farmer had a heart attack. Then I was busy doing all the farm chores by myself.

One day my mail carrier delivered a huge envelope with letters from every one of that class of little Denver students. They drew pictures and wrote consoling notes. Several said, "Here are pictures to make you smile." I laughed and smiled with tears running down my face. I feel Farmer and I made a difference in their lives. I know they surely helped me.

WHEEL CHAIR OLYMPICS

High jump standout for Chadron State College and Thedford High School, brother Jim is competing again. Jim was injured on March 1, 1983 when his horse rolled on him and has been wheelchair bound ever since. He lost his right hand in a corn picker in 1971 so he uses his left hand. Jim, who spent two years in the army in Korea after graduation, was one of 600 paralyzed veterans participating in the National Paralyzed Veterans' Wheel Chair Olympics in Omaha. Each veteran was limited to five events.

Jim's placed first in the Novice Archery with a compound Bow and Ping-Pong earning gold medals. He received second place in Field Discus throw, Slalom novice maneuvering around cones, time 4.16.25, and Novice Air Gun Para for three silver medals. He met paralyzed veterans from all over the U.S. and enjoyed the experience. Volunteers took pictures and assisted with events and lodging. "We were treated wonderfully; their help was great," he said. Jim especially enjoyed visiting with Scott, a veteran injured in Iraq in 2003 who holds the world record for discus and javelin throw. He will be in the U.S. Para-Olympics Track and Field National Championships in Beijing, China next. Scott captured gold medals in shot, discus and javelin in Omaha. Jim appreciated Tony, who gave him a neck-shoulder massage that relieved tightness which has bothered 25 years. "Now I can turn my head," Jim said.

Cheering for Jim was his son Tim, a Marine veteran, grandson Dustin and three year old granddaughter, Taylor Ann who yelled, "Go, Grandpa Go!"

The next challenge for Jim is locating a publisher for his family research. He has collected pictures and documented family stories of our Grandpa Claude S. Paine and other family members as far back as the Civil War veterans.

TRIBUTE TO JOHN

My life was full of happiness and joy and a moment later my world fell apart. On May 10, 2007. I was substitute teaching and enjoying my family. I taught Kindergarten in Chadron and drove to visit John and Alyssa. John coaxed, "Stay for snack and visit. Alyssa has things to show you."

The next day a friend invited me to her house to meet guests and to stay for supper. We had a nice time, though I thought, 'I forgot my cell; I should check my home phone. No, That would be rude—no one calls me in afternoons.' On the way home, a ten mile drive on twisty roads, I felt an urgency to hurry. My phone was ringing when I opened the door. I rushed to answer. My quiet older son exclaimed, "Where have you been?" I have always told my family, "Always let someone know where you are." I had violated my rule and felt guilty.

Jerry's next words shook me! He said, "I have bad news. It's about John." I asked, "What John?" I though, 'Our John is home safe; I just saw him.' Jerry told me both he and Wayne had tried all afternoon to reach me—'every five minutes.' My car license was on the State Patrol's list to locate. The Patrol had driven to my house and called. No one knew where I was. Jerry commanded, "Stay where you are, I am coming to get you." He kept talking the next 45 minutes as he drove to my house.

I felt the air knocked out of me—hard; I gasped realizing he was referring to John Snyder, my son-in-law. John had gone for an old truck he'd bought and had fixed to make their home safe from trees and future fires. He had looked under the truck box and it dropped on him! I listened gasping for breath. "Our John, gone! "Oh, No!!" My world and that of my family has turned upside down. There are lots of helpful people but a tiny little girl has lost her Daddy. She is now afraid to let her Mom or Grandma out of sight.

How long this will last and what the future holds is known but to God. The service was a testimony to a quiet helpful young man who loved God, family and friends. There were tears by many including his pastor friend, Steve Moody. A tremendous turn out of people and flowers showed love and respect for John. Kristi requested memorials for Alyssa's education. John helped many with his faith shining. He planned to come to my house the next day to help me move shelves of little pitchers and old dishes.

He left a legacy of love for Alyssa; he taught her to fold her little hands and pray to thank God for food, family and friends. Alyssa remembers. Her mother helps by sharing pictures and stories of John. Alyssa tells everyone, "My Daddy is in Heaven."

Jerry drove to take me to Kristi's house. Friends gathered with hugs and tears when I entered her home. Missy and Nancy were there, having driven from Rapid City. We three stayed all night. I spent that night and many more with my daughter and three year old granddaughter. My younger son Wayne, drove me home a week later to check on animals and to get my car.

Widowed at 55, I thought I was much too young to be left alone. Now my daughter faced the same fate years younger. I try to help. We are country survivors.

My faith in the goodness of many people grows as I turn my tomorrows over to Him. Last year my house was broken into and valuable family heirlooms stolen. I am putting problems in perspective and looking toward better days. I am thankful my son and his wife didn't bump into the robbers armed for anything. The robbers came back two weeks later and cut a big new padlock on my gate taking another large load of family tools and treasures!

Our family is close; they call more often. I know what it is like to loose loved ones. I have two grandsons and many family waiting in heaven. We look forward to meeting beyond this life. Alyssa said, "I want to go to Heaven now. Why can't we drive there?" My faith grows as I continue to commit my children and grandchildren to God's protection. I pray for them often. I believe God uses us through experiences so we can comfort others.

The sun still shines but our lives are tinted with loss. We will never be the same for one we loved entered the Pearly Gates to wait. There is a big hole in the family. John is greatly missed, his goodness lives on. We hear reports of others who he has helped anonymously.

Two months passed and Kristi called before 5 in the morning July 5, requesting a ride to hospital emergency room saying she has unbearable pain. She had emergency surgery for a ruptured gall bladder requiring many stitches and two units of blood. Separation scared Alyssa, she asked, "Will my Mommy come home?" She refused to go near her mother until she was sure she is coming home from the hospital. We are strong in faith and endurance.

PERSPECTIVE

COMPARING

"If you haven't grown up by the time you are 40 you don't have to," is an appealing adage. Our world has changed so much in the past 60 or 70 years it amazes me. What does the future will hold? A household was supported with one income and wife/mother stayed home and took care of children, cooked, cleaned, chores and more. Gold was $35 an ounce. Dow Jones was 107.

Today the median household income in Nebraska is around $40,000 with both husband and wife working for wages. I wish! We learn to get by on less. New homes cost $138,000.

Average price of a new vehicle is reported to be $26,000 or more which is about half a yearly income. Each family member needs a vehicle since both work. Price of gas in the old days was 10 to 21 cents a gallon up to 80 cents a gallon. What happened? Gas doesn't change! Who is filling pockets? I think it was around 30 cents a gallon when my brothers and I drove to high school every day. We were happy to be home on nights and weekends. Is it any wonder I shuddered today when I had to pay $3.69 for a gallon of gas. Driving is a necessity in todays society. It isn't the rancher or farmer getting rich. Farm and ranch wives hold jobs in town to help finance the fuel for their operation.

When we compare the price of what things cost 70 years ago: an average new house cost $4,100.00, average wages per year $1,780.00, cost of a gallon of gas was 10 cents, house rent was $26.00 per month, a loaf of bread was nine cents, a pound of hamburger meat was 12 cents, price for new car was $760.00. Toothpaste cost 35 cents.

We raised our own beef and had plenty. Our mother baked fresh bread every few days to keep a supply. She had a 50 or 100 pound sacks of flour for baking. She made biscuits, fry bread and cinnamon rolls too. Neighbors worked together to butcher.

Dad said he paid more in taxes on his place than he did buying it at $5.00 an acre in 1936. The seller was in a hurry for his money. Dad kept a letter requesting pay earlier than agreed to buy a home out west. Traveling, we were crowded in the pickup to attend a school program. Dad drove to town when he needed repairs or supplies we didn't have or to sell a pig. Once my folks bought new snap clothes pins. My sister and brothers clipped them all over my hair. When Grandpa stopped in, my siblings disappeared, leaving me with a 'pinned up hair..'

Camaraderie and fellowship in our family continue after all these years for which I am thankful. We didn't know others had more or traveled in newer cars. It didn't matter, we were blessed with love and understanding parents who kept us involved making work fun on the ranch. Years of expenses and living have changed but love of family breathes deep and continues to circulate through our veins. Faith in the God of the Bible will lead us on the right path. Our perspective makes the difference.

WOMEN AND PEACE

Women have a tradition of filling in where needed and making a difference for their family, those around them. When we feel the need, we stand up to be counted to make changes happen. My Great Grandmother Elizabeth Kathryn Lewellen Burris Giles helped make hospital gowns during the first world war and used the tiny scraps leftover to piece the back of a quilt for her family.

Military efforts involve working together with civilian men and women. The Denton Journal of Maryland reported, June 6, 1942, "Throughout the country it is estimated that 1,000,000 more women will have to go into industry during 1942." It continues, "No battle in any part of the world can take place without involving us. Here at home we must drive toward victory. We must take and maintain an unrelenting offensive. Here at home we must hew the wood and carry the water for rebuilding of a triumphant peace."

Young US women joined forces to work in defense and learning skills they had never tried before. Women used homemaking skills in ways no one would have expected for the peace effort. While sons and husbands were far away involved in war, women got busy in industrial work on the home front. They planned and drew, then sewed patriotic designs using a liberty bell, eagles, red, white and blue stars and stripes on quilts to encourage patriotism of our military forces.

Postage stamps showed a large V for victory. Schools sold victory stamps to raise money savings bonds. We collected foil and newspapers to donate. Our school participated by gathering foil and dandelion fluff for making parachutes for soldiers. We took contributions to school to fill boxes for soldiers. We filled numerous boxes for soldiers by sending toothpaste, combs, towels, soap, tooth brushes, wash cloths, nail clippers, handkerchiefs, little books, writing paper and envelopes for soldiers. Our mother generously promoted helping the military.

There is a history of women being relegated as, "just a homemaker." For years our income tax report listed me as "homemaker," and nothing more though I was, in fact a mother, substitute teacher and doing a lot of other jobs on the farm. I enjoy choices some women have never had. I liked helping my husband in the fields and working with our children plus meeting and helping students in town and in country schools throughout Sioux and Dawes County. Women are capable and can do much more than they were once allowed.

Our favorite picture: four grandsons holding puppies beside the barn. Andy, Will, Cody and Joey.

PANHANDLE LIVING

SUDDENLY ALONE

For years I worked beside my husband helping on the family farm. We shared work and caring for our children. We were best friends. On May 18, 1992, I had a sore throat so he went alone to check the tank for watering cattle. He returned laying on the horn saying, "I'm terribly sick! Shut the gate." He wobbled walking to the door while I ran to shut the gate. I rushed back to find him on the sofa. I asked about calling the ambulance. He said, "No!" I didn't want to upset him so I waited then checked him again. His eyes were fixed! I called 911 and began CPR. I continued CPR while holding the phone to my ear until the ambulance arrived. I followed the ambulance alone in my car after shutting the yard gate. I slid, nearly going off the road speeding on a corner.

Wayne, Julie, Cody and baby Ashley met me at the hospital. The doctor came out in a minute and said, "He's gone." A kind nurse brought a chair so I wouldn't fall. Life, as I'd known it, was over. Soon Jerry, Kathy, Andy, Will and Joey hurriedly drove from Scottsbluff offering hugs and encouragement as we shared our sorrow. Kristi drove from Rapid City. We were all in shock and in deep grief. The next day a cow needed a C-section so Jerry and Wayne loaded her in the pickup driving to the veterinary who delivered the calf. We all stood and watched with tears in our eyes. I commented, "God knew we needed a distraction." Jerry and Wayne hauled the pigs to market shortly thereafter.

After the service my family left for home and work. I was completely alone for the first time in my life. Rains began. Harold had been upset over drought and worried over his crops. There was nothing to do now but wait to farm. I did chores, chased cattle, fixed fence and came inside wiping back my many tears.

Farming each morning was the same. I rose early and cooked oat meal cereal, after pulling on my faded jeans and a long-sleeved shirt. I chased cattle, fed chickens, filled the tractor tank, checked oil and greased machinery. I put on a cap and spent daylight to dark, turning over summer fallow. I took along a water jug and an orange and kept going. Tears flowed freely in the tractor cab as I prayed. I thought, I am too young to be a widow, but thinking doesn't change facts. Work must be done and there is no one here but me to do it.

The dogs treed a raccoon and barked a lot. In daylight, I shot several raccoon. If the coon fell while Aric and Brownie guarded, they grabbed it. I didn't go out after dark; I knew it could be a rattlesnake. We had shot rattlesnakes in the yard. But now I couldn't hold the light and the gun at the same time.

Baby, the bottle-fed calf, went where he wanted. I called him Baby so he wouldn't have a real name and we wouldn't get attached to him. Little grandsons loved feeding Baby when he was a small calf but now he had bonded to me. He butted me when he was hungry. He was huge and I was afraid of him. He started going through the gate on the road. He couldn't be shooed. I moved him with a feed bucket— if he was hungry. Late one night a neighbor called, "There's a black cow on the road." It was Baby. I told neighbor I was afraid of Baby and couldn't get him in alone. "Click!" He hung up!

Julie helped fix fence and did some mowing. Alfalfa was drying. A friend called offering to help. After numerous bruises trying to hitch the mower, I accepted. I didn't need broken bones and I never could mow square corners. Friend mowed but I raked and stacked. Harold had told me, "Operating a farmhand is a mans work." It was a struggle but I made some decent haystacks. Hydraulic needed filled, teeth straightened; it was hot dusty work. I kept up until hay was stacked. I was actually thankful there wasn't a lot of hay.

Each night I came in after dark, covered with dirt and dusty tear stains to an empty house. Brown Dog wagged and Aric crowded close in the pickup. Aric transferred his devotion to me. He shadowed me and I needed his company. There was no lack of work. I was so tired I slept—some. When I woke in the dark hours of night, I prayed, cried and wrote in my notebook.

Sundays were horrible. I attended Sunday School and church and wondered, "What next?" Sunday afternoons are endless. On weekdays I drilled wheat and kept busy with many chores. In winter there was ice to chop and little else to fill my hours. The lonely hurt continues.

I believe people appear to shun widows because they: 1) don't want to see tears, 2) don't know what to say, 3) are busy with families, 4) don't think of them, 5) don't care, 6) feel uncomfortable near them, and 7) are afraid of gossip. Maybe all of the above.

Widows are the most lonesome, misunderstood people I know. Only other widows can relate to a flood of tears at a picture, a thought or a tune. It takes so long to feel whole again. A comment can make you fall to pieces. I still miss my love. The hardest part is being alone.

A month later son Wayne drove in at 7 A.M. to find me on a tractor farming in a field near the house. He said, "Kristi and John have been in an accident. Do you want to go see them?" They were coming see me so, of course, I wanted to see them. We arrived in the emergency room 125 miles away to find them still on stretchers. John had a bad cuts near his eye and shoulder. I held his hand as the doctor sewed. We waited in the emergency room until after 5 P.M. John and Kristi had broken backs and she had a shattered shoulder blade. We hadn't eaten since breakfast and didn't think of food. I stayed in Rapid, spending my days at the hospital for four weeks until it was wheat harvest time. Doctors said they didn't know if either John or Kristi would walk again. Finally, they walked out wearing back braces.

For five seasons I farmed alone cultivating summer fallow and putting in over a hundred acres of wheat each fall besides putting up hay. During the first season, the biggest tire of the biggest tractor went flat. I wondered what next? I called a repair man in town to fix my monster sized fluid filled tractor tire.

I sold the cattle that first fall because, I reasoned, they were too tame to feed on the place. They ate cubes from my hands and I thought how it would be to get knocked down with no one around. I took some hay to them in the sale barn corrals. Tears ran down my face as I watched them go through the sale ring. After that I sold hay on the place.

Jerry and Wayne hauled Baby to the sale barn. It was a relief to have him gone because he had become dangerous. My Dad called one morning asking how I was doing. I cried, I didn't know how to sort cows. My 80 year old father drove 200 miles to help me fix fence and sort cattle for turning them to pasture that same day. My mother, not in good health, waited in the house while we worked sorting and fixing fence. I wiped tears of gratitude from my eyes when I saw them at the gate coming to help me.

The dogs barked until I went out under the yard light and killed a big rattlesnake by the front yard gate one dark night with a spade. I lost 42 pounds farming alone. I continued to substitute teach and began training and working with Shari Meyer in Extension Service during winter months doing school enrichment programs all over the county and in extended counties. I did GED and ASFAB testing for a number of years.

In 1991, I began writing to my niece's students in Denver, telling what it was like living on the farm. I told them about My Farmer, the animals and the varied hard work he did every day to feed and care for our animals. They wrote back and asked a multitude of questions about living and working in the country. We had good communication and enjoyed exchanging letters. Then I quit. Glenda, my niece, knew what happened. Several weeks later I found in my mailbox the nicest over sized envelope containing the sweetest letters and drawings by these caring little students. They drew bright pictures and many wrote, "Here are pictures to make you smile." I smiled through my tears.

Ruth, my mail carrier, stopped one morning when I met her at the mailbox. She gave me a big hug and said, "I wanted you to know, you have received more cards the past several months than anyone I know." Several years later she called me late one evening asking how she could be assured of reaching heaven. She was on oxygen and not well. I quoted some scripture like: I John 1:9, "Believe on the Lord Jesus Christ and you will be saved." She prayed then said, "Thank you, I feel better already." I was touched, feeling my heartache helped her.

FAMILY REUNION

We love a family gathering
Tho reunion times are rare
We have much to talk about
We have lots to share.

We meet loved ones
We have long known
How long, we leave untold
No names, but some are old.

We meet our loved ones
We've not seen—for years.
Reunion time is a time of fun
But we may shed some tears.

We miss ones who are gone
Their earthly life is o'er
Through God's grace
We'll meet and see His face.

Welcome you who've joined
By way of wedding vow
We may seem odd, but persevere
You're in the family now!

We're glad to see little ones
They put on quite a show
As we let them entertain us
We should younger grow.

When parting time comes
Good byes are hard, we know
We hope to meet again
If God ordains it so.
Christ died to save us from sins
If we, in Him believe and love
We'll live in Heaven with Christ
We'll meet for a reunion above!

THE GIFT

My daughter Kristi handed me a lovely wrapped box containing a bright red and pink floral housecoat. The gift was a symbol of love and caring from her for my birthday.

The robe brought comfort now three months later, in June. Kristi has a way of choosing the "just right" gifts. This time I had actually wondered about the robe when I unwrapped it. I was too big for the robe to fit on my birthday. Besides, I am a country homemaker and rarely wear a robe. My old blue robe was bought to wear in the hospital years earlier when she was born.

In June, three months after my birthday, as a widow, I had lost a lot of weight. The robe felt good to tie the sash comfortably around my slim waist. I needed the bright lightweight robe to spend nights with a friend near the hospital. My daughter was flat on her back with a broken back and shoulder-blade, well over a hundred miles from home. Her fiance' was in the next hospital room with a broken back also.

Kristi and John were coming to visit me, because I needed company since her father's sudden death. Now I was needed to stay by them in the hospital. Doctors said they didn't know if either John or Kristi would ever walk again. John's pickup hydroplaned and flipped end for end as they were driving so see me to bring the comfort of their company. I wore that bright robe at my friend's home daily for the month they were hospitalized.

I watched John and Kristi's eyes brighten when the nurses decided to roll his bed into the doorway of her room. This was the first they saw each other since breaking their backs weeks earlier. It felt good to see them rejuvenated by the visit. I believe Kristi is in tune with a higher power source when it comes to knowing what I needed before I had need of it. I didn't know I would ever wear a bright floral robe. Kristi and God knew even though I did not, she seems to have have a gift of giving.

RED ROSE

The large rose was perfect in every way, a brilliant beautiful red blossom blooming in my yard. Red was my husband Harold's favorite color. And the rose was an answer to my prayer.

I was praying for evidence of God's power and presence while driving the long lonely road home from Rapid City to take care of business—final bills. I was visiting our youngest, daughter and her fiance', in the hospital in Rapid City where both lay with broken backs.

Tears blurred my eyes and ran down my cheeks as I wiped them away and kept driving. I was trying to draw courage to face this empty home alone. Nothing is more lonesome than facing an empty home for the first time alone. How could I know for certain that my beloved husband was resting safe in the arms of Jesus?

I prayed, asking for a symbol of reassurance that Harold was with Jesus in Heaven. I found my reassurance in that beautiful red rose. My love and I had planted that rose plant together not 30 days earlier. As it turned out it was a few days before his sudden unexpected fatal heart attack. The rose bloomed with one big beautiful red blossom. No one saw that flower but me— and it never bloomed again. The rose was an answer to my prayer.

BUTTERFLY

"Did you know butterflies were Georgia's favorite symbol for eternal life?" Kristi, my daughter asked as we left the cemetery that afternoon after committal services. I didn't know but I had made a computer card for Georgia's husband with butterflies. They seemed appropriate then, after the services, I noticed there were many colorful butterflies flying near by as we walked across the road with friends to our vehicles parked away from the grave site.

Kristi explained, "Georgia had a box of butterflies she loved, given to her by a friend." We believe the Lord does direct our actions, when we let Him. I was thankful I had followed through and made a butterfly card to remember a special shared cancer stricken friend.

Jerry, Wayne, their father Harold and baby Kristi dressed up for a wedding in 1971.

MY ANGELS

Angels, I am told, can come any time and in any form. A private angel came to my home, bringing his young daughter along. He worked hard chopping heavy thick ice out of a stock tank. I was genuinely grateful as I had tried chopping that ice and couldn't even crack it. He quietly refused to accept any pay or anything beyond a sincere "Thank you."

A few years earlier, an angel came out of a repair shop when my car started boiling over. I, a recent widow, drove to the repair shop in panic asking, "What do I need for a leaking radiator?" The salesman handed me the necessary hose and an elderly angel in denim quietly walked outside and said, "I know how to put that hose on." He quickly put on the new radiator hose that fixed the problem. I will always remember the kindness of that angel though I don't even know his name. I hope he realized how much his help meant to me.

Other angels have been available to help when a tractor broke down and when a tire went flat. A machinery wheel came off so an angel drove out to fix the problem. Angels can be unidentified but they special in many ways.

Some angels are my sons and daughter and their spouses who call or show up to help and offer encouragement when I need it most. There are times I really do need help with projects. I can do a lot but some things are beyond my abilities. I was a farm helper. My daughter loves to cook and occasionally brings a casserole with side dishes for a shared meal. I enjoy playing with grandchildren while their parents help with the work I don't know how to do.

My grandsons are encouraging and helpful when they come. I was upset, several years ago, then young grandson offered, "Don't worry, Grandma, I will help you." He sincerely meant it. He came out and did some fence fixing recently.

There are always jobs that need assistance in the country. My son-in-law was helpful on some jobs. My daughter-in-law was here to drive the rake tractor and fix fence back when I needed so much help. She was a beautiful angel wearing blue denim.

I was lost was in Rapid City one night, after a day in the hospital with Kristi and John in June 1992. I had street names on a paper but I couldn't find them. I am near sighted and signs don't show up at night. Add tears and rain blurring my vision a month after Harold's heart attack. Cars were impatient following me— a lost driver. Some ladies came along and said, "Follow us." I was so thankful for those angels.

Angles come in many forms and can be seen or not. Some angels are seen briefly while some are just sensed. I know my angels were real and they were greatly appreciated. God bless them for the many good things they do for others.

BLANK BOOK

A favorite book in our family is an old 'World History' book with absolutely nothing printed on the pages inside. I found the book in an old book case and began sharing it with my young children. The little ones and I drew pictures and wrote stories and poems. Each of the children and later the grandchildren traced their hands and composed what they wanted in 'our book.'

Gramps did some interesting drawings in 'our book.' I wrote stories about our little boys setting traps with their father in the pine covered picturesque hills complete with illustrations of them and the skunk they caught. We wrote stories about their animals and adventures. They learned to read with those silly stories. We wrote rhyming stories and fun tongue twisters. I wrote some stories of their adventures real and imagined. There is a picture of their father drawn by each child and grandchild. Some books become valuable to the owners by what they have entered inside themselves. Our blank book is such a book. It is a fun book to look at. I wrote numerous stories which we often read. We all like our blank book.

TRAVELS

LONDON

Cultural shock! The loud noises and multitudes of people, 13.5 million of them, were a bombardment to my senses when we landed in London. I couldn't sleep for the constant sirens, police and ambulance, cars and buses roaring past all night. Breakfast chatter was in every language, and none I recognized. Continual loud noises strained my ears.

Many strangers were impeccably fashionably well dressed in suits and ties. Women wore beautiful dresses and splendid large brimmed hats. In rural Nebraska we are informal and quiet. I am not accustomed to constant racket.

Wide open spaces with the sound of wind, coyote's howling at night and birds, with a distant train are the sum of my noise experiences. I appreciate my family, space and the green grass of home all the more since being in London. It was nice to go to the Post Office and see people I knew instead of a mass of strangers rushing past.

London has kind helpful people that I met while out and about. When I turned my ankle and fell while walking on a busy street, there was an instant group of people of all descriptions offering to help and suggesting I sit out a spell. There were no benches so I kept walking—at a slower pace. Some kind workers took off to show the next bus stop. A young worker went out of his way to walk several blocks until he was sure I knew where to go.

Elderly ladies out on 'a holiday' walked with us and talked about the sites. They stayed in contact until they, and we, found the next bus stop. A man from Wales gave directions to an Underground Railroad, 'tube stop.' "We weren't lost, just having adventures." An Australian tourist offered to take our picture in the London Eye. He laughed and said to me, "You look fetching" in the funny glasses while watching a four dimension preview movie before the ride. I appreciated the guard explaining the meaning of each activity at Buckingham Palace during changing of the guards. A curator at Guard Museum offered to take pictures with a wax guard figure. A friendly lady from Cambridge showed me in the museum, a quote from an English soldier who wrote, "I was surprised at how nice the Americans soldiers were to us after they beat us at the Boston Tea Party." People are kind though they do speak up. A cute young Australian showed off for Ashley. When he left he called out, "You are beautiful."

IMPRESSIVE SITES VISITED

Oxford has 59 colleges with huge imposing buildings surrounded by perfect grass, which they do not permit anyone to walk on. The college motto is "God is my Light." There were marble busts of many past leaders. Students were studying quietly. There aren't adjectives enough to describe the massive ornate old buildings.

We visited Stratford Upon Avon, the house where William Shakespeare was born in 1564 as a group. We climbed the old brick stairs to the upstairs in the house where he lived as a child and helped his father make gloves. The bed was set up in his parent's bedroom with a fireplace showing smoke of hundreds of years ago. "He is buried deep in the area nearby," the curator explained. Castle education began in 1058 with monks as fine teachers. The time seems impossible to comprehend. We were told that the Royal Air Force is still active. There are legends of a ghost haunt in the state rooms of the college. We learned, "The protectors of the castle would catapult bee hives from up high to stop invading knights."

Warwick Castle, was built in 1066, the year William the Conqueror came into power. William had many children who fought over his estate and the right to reign when he died 'of old age' at age 59 years. Warwick Castle has many turrets and a history of crime, mystery, cruelty and princes. There were wax figures and people in costumes depicting some of the soldiers and activities in the castle. Warwick is a pretty castle. We visited some characters dressed up inside the castle. They were fun to talk to and enjoyed getting their picture taken.

The British History Museum portrays a history of the world with ancient objects. Many were carvings in rock 'beginning about 40,000 years ago.' Enormous wall carvings from Israel and the holy lands surprised me. There were huge statues carved thousands of years ago to represent era history. Clocks through the years and money of various kinds were displayed. I took a picture of a carving showing Jonah and Nineveh.

An Underground rail pass, 'oyster', took us to Piccadilly Station where we walked to spend two hours in Ripley's Believe it or not and a Mirror Maze. Many amazing exhibits were of torture. Wax figures, like the tallest man, seven foot and American heroes. A car painted with Mount Rushmore, a blow up bra, plus Elvis and Marilyn Monroe exhibits, were among those on display. "Dazzling Dirty Dancing" a live play production was impressive. The props and scenery were good as was the acting, lights and set effects.

Hyde Park was interesting. I took pictures of monuments, arches, statues and flowering shrubs. I had to laugh about "The David" who the tour guide on the bus said was turned away from traffic because it caused too many crashes when facing the street.

Windsor Castle was our destination for Sunday. A red headed lady beside us on the tube ride had just completed a Marathon race in Manchester and won! Her husband said he ran with her the last three miles. Her feet hurt so badly she was still barefoot when she got off at their stop. We saw Queen Victoria and Albert's art collections, the Queen Mary's big doll house, details were tiny and exquisite. It was dark inside but we walked around and looked. I liked the Albert and Victoria family painting and large dolls with elegant clothing. There were enormous paintings and delicate gold trimmed dishes. We saw exquisite crowns and jewelery. A golden grand piano the royalty once used was on display. We stopped in a little gift shop after touring Windsor Castle and saw three teams of horses driving in below. The young clerk screamed, "There's the Queen!" She said the first driver was Prince Phillip. The clerk and all around rushed outside to a brick wall to watch. We captured pictures of the Queen wearing a bright red coat touching the noses of the first team of horses.

Buckingham Palace was a disappointment when we went to see the changing of the guard. We couldn't get close enough to see anything; many heads crowded close in front of us. Every picture I took has strangers blocking my view. We left and looked around Saint James Park, across the way we noticed large statues. Several days later we were told to dress more formally then were delighted to be informed we would go inside the palace gates to witness changing of the guard from next to Buckingham Palace with a guard explaining the entire ceremony. I reached back and touched

Buckingham Palace! Pictures were not allowed so we kept our eyes open wide taking in proceedings.

The National Gallery had huge paintings by famous artists. I liked best a royal family painting that took 12 years to complete. Many were gruesome like John the Baptist's head. We liked statues outside and the fountain. Monet, Van Gogh and naked models are not favorites.

Saint Martin-in-the-Fields Church was ornate, tall and massive. A lady was practicing her violin. We later learned she was to be a guest performer in a day or two. The music was beautiful. The church was huge and amazing. There were kneeling benches for each individual. There were cubicles in the sides with their own kneeling benches. The church was built in 1726 and is still impressive and well maintained today.

A tube ride to Westminster Abbey was worthwhile. We arrived as there were many dignitaries coming out the front gate from a service. Ladies wore extremely elegant dresses, jewelery and beautiful large brimmed hats. The men wore military uniforms decorated with ropes and medals. I snapped many pictures. I overheard someone say it was a memorial service for Lord Koker of the Chilean Navy. After the people left we were allowed inside a side door. We wandered around seeing numerous ancient crypts of important people of the past. The tomb of their unknown Soldier was buried in the floor on November 11, 1920. Darwin, Handel, Elizabeth I, Queen Mary (Is this 'Blood Mary?') and others are entombed in the church. Some had likenesses carved on their crypt. A touching one was of two infants on a small crypt.

Guard Museum was interesting. That's where I met Marjorie Butler of Cambridge who made sure I saw the quote of an English soldier admiring the kindness of Americans toward them after the Boston Tea Party defeat. There are models, uniforms, ammunition, spears, guns, pictures and medals with information from every conflict including new ones from Iraq and Afghanistan. There are models of soldiers outside the museum. The curator said his position is volunteer. He served as a soldier was knowledgable of the museum and battles.

The Curiosity Shop, made famous by author Charles Dickens, was an interesting surprise. It is tiny with not much inside but some very expensive shoes for sale. The lady said she does not allow pictures. I took one outside before we went inside.

The college group took a Jack the Ripper tour one evening. It was a chilling experience. I had heard of him but did not know details of his horrible deeds. The dark shadowy old walls made it real though it happened hundreds of years before. The guide did a good job bringing the story to life with gruesome information. Criminal Justice students were puzzling over what must have happened and why. No one knows details of the still unsolved mystery.

Cambridge, location of many colleges and the Cam River, was fun. We took a leisure punting ride on the river to photograph many colleges and beautiful old historic bridges along the route. Our guide, 18 year old Peter, told details of each view. He said, "England doesn't have graduation from high school." He will complete his basic education after two more classes and be ready for college. He said he doesn't want to attend in Cambridge. Their library is near the river and does not have any books on the lower level to protect them from flood damage. The river was quiet and there were people strolling, picnicking and resting along the route. We saw a huge old church where we signed up for the punting trip.

Prime Minister of London resigned while we were there. A group of college students took a fast walk to #10 Downey street to see the home of the former Prime Minister. We passed through security and were allowed to get our pictures taken at the #10 door. There were a few people coming in 'to present claims' the guide said. I collected signatures of a young guard and Metropolitan Policeman. They were kind and explained what was happening. Pictures were not allowed toward the security doors to protect their location.

The Medieval Supper was loud but interesting. We were seated next to four Omaha boys who appreciated visiting, passing food and sharing. They signed my journal and enjoyed themselves. I was glad to get out of the noise and back on the Underground Tube, headed for the hotel room for one last night. We were among the first to leave and still it was midnight when we pulled up the covers.

Impressions of London were awe at the numerous beautiful marble churches. The people have done a wonderful of job preserving their heritage for future generations. I am thankful to be home living free from monarchy. Nebraska looks great. I am content to stay and to teach young students. London was a unique experience for my memory bank. I have numerous pictures of the experience to share.

Great Grandmother Margaret Tindale Vasey told of her ancestors coming to England with William the Conquerer who was mentioned in London. The Vasey family came from England and returned in 1907 when they found the old castle in ruins. They were thankful they had come to America to live.

Grandma told me her mother said she was related to William Tyndale who translated the Bible into English, which became the King James version of the Bible published in 1611— 400 years ago. Tyndale was educated in Oxford and Cambridge and was fluent in eight languages. He had no descendants. A connection to Thomas Paine through Grandpa Paine was denied by Grandma. I found an old letter from his cousin which said, "Yes, we are related to Thomas Paine, I will tell you how someday." She added, "His name is now used to scare naughty children." The media abused him, who had no descendants. Research indicates he did much good and was not the atheist portrayed. He wrote 'Common Sense' which George Washington ordered printed 'for every soldier.' The publication turned the tide in the Revolutionary War and became the most widely distributed writing per capita. Like Jack the Ripper stories, the media was looking for ways to generate newspaper sales. Jack the Ripper, a brutal character, was never caught.

WORLD TRAVEL

My family grew up isolated so far out in the country, that it truly amazes me that we have traveled as we have the past several decades. Brother Jim served in communication in the Army in Korea in 1958-1960. He visited in orphanages and the lonesome hills around Seoul. His son Tim served as a Marine truck driver in Korea.

Daughter Kristi and John took a college business tour to England in 1995 which included London castles, Mount Titliss in Switzerland, a train trip to Scarborough and a taxi ride to explore Brompton. They took many pictures to show and share where her Great Grandma was born.

Son Wayne and granddaughter Ashley flew to Norway in 2002 to help as volunteer missionary workers. They spent over a week and toured a big museum that showed Norwegian sailing vessels.

Grandson Cody was selected by the Eisenhower initiated 'People to People' wrestling exchange to wrestle in New Zealand and Australia, accompanied by his father. He donated his wrestling sling to a student there. Cody spent time in Germany and Iraq in the Army. He and his wife Tonya toured Italy, Austria, France and Switzerland with Baby Carson. They explored Neuschwanstein Castle, Dachau and a salt mine in Germany. Christmas 2008, Wayne, Julie and Ashley visited Cody,Tonya and little Carson in Germany seeing castles and churches of interest.

Son Jerry flew to Bucharest, Romania to adopt five year old Mindy in 1998. She got sick on the train and was admitted to a hospital for several days. His guide showed them a museum and interesting sites. In 2001, I flew with Jerry to Bucharest to get seven year old Ana. Ana thought she was in America in a sparse apartment up many flights of stairs with a Daddy, Grandma and a suitcase full of hair pretties, clothes and shoes her parents had bought for her. Our translator Beebe, drove us to a store, museum, hospital and the American Embassy where we stood in line for adoption clearance in Bucharest. The Embassy was impressive with marble steps and walls. Jerry photographed the New York twin towers on our return trip just six weeks before 9-11. Jerry and Kathy flew to Moscow to adopt Ivan, seven and Ben,18 months in 2003. They flew to Estonia to adopt Marina,16, who had cried for a family, in 2006. Kathy flew to China in 2008, to adopt Jade, three years old. Kathy was required to spend two weeks with Jade in China before returning home.

In 2004, I saw Manchester, England where Great Grandmother Margaret Tindale Vasey was born, attended girls' school and worked in a factory. I took pictures of young school girls in school uniforms. I traveled to Brompton where my Grandma Vasey Paine was born and found the house where she lived. She had shared old picture postcards of their home and the church. I photographed the huge picturesque church inside and out where Grandma was christened at two weeks and her parents were married years earlier. I walked up a lane to go in and around the very old church in Ebberston, where Great Grandpa George Vasey's parents, Thomas and Hannah Dowsland Vasey were married. I walked in a damp moss covered cemetery in Wykham and found a tomb stone belonging to Hannah's father, Francis Dowsland. I climbed a steep path to view castle remnants in Scarborough and the Scarborough docks, where the Vasey family left to set sail for America in 1883. I saw the Queen's residence, toured veterinarian, James Harriott's clinic, saw Paris, Arch of Triumph and rode an elevator high in the Eiffel Tower. I met young Pakistani, Aiman and Fatima Hussain who wrote and spoke perfect English. They signed my little book with their names, birthdays and address, They were 'on holiday' in a London hotel. I saw Neuschwanstein Castle in Bavaria, walked around the Dachau Holocaust with Photographer Gary Morgan of Wales. He later shared pictures of Dachau. I was in the enormous Saint Francis of Assisi Memorial Church.

In 2005 I traveled to Esslingen, Germany where Granddaddy Weber was born. I saw the Salzburg Salt Mine and a Dome over the jail where Paul of the Bible wrote from prison in Rome. I sailed in a Gondola in Venice, took an air boat to Cairo, walked in Florence, saw The Coliseum and Roman Road. I watched Pope John II at the Vatican. I saw ancient Pompeii drawings, ruins and remains of volcano ash fallout from 79 AD and rediscovered in 1748.

Then I pause and remember, Granddaddy Weber came to America at age two with his family from Germany in 1879. Grandma Paine sailed at 20 months with her parents and siblings plus their aunts, uncles and grandparents from England landing in New York on April 22, 1883. Many other ancestors came earlier traveling from the United Kingdom and I don't know where. People travel all over the world and have for centuries.

Gibbons Family Century Farm Ranch recognition: front; Kristi and Alyssa, Ben, Jerry and Will. middle; Kathy, Jade. Ivan, Mindy and Ana. back; Julie, Wayne, Beth, Cody, Tonya and Carson. Absent were: Andy, Dawn, Joey and Addie, Ashley, Marina and Lyman.

CONCLUSION

This book was written to share memories of faith, hope, love and respect for family and our ancestors who lived in the isolated sand covered hills and the panhandle of Nebraska. It is from my perspective, as I have lived and worked in the country. I have great respect for my many ancestors and how they survived. Today's advancements in communication are useful but they leave no information trail for future generations. I feel that I am blessed to have known my children, grandchildren and great grandchildren. Little Joe and tiny Gabriel are in Heaven with their grandfathers waiting for a grand reunion. I look forward to seeing them, believing Acts 16:31, "Believe in the Lord Jesus and you will be saved." Joe's favorite verse was Isaiah 40:31. Joe declared he was healed of the Lord but he was healed to heaven, not on this earth. My memories of living in the Nebraska Sandhills and Panhandle linger. I believe it is time to share. I wrote for my family and for future generations. I am sharing a kaleidoscope of adventures with the sincere hope of preserving a trail of the character strength, faith and endurance of these gentle quiet hard working people who we call family.

SANDHILLS SUNSHINE

My Grandparents lived in the Sandhills,
Living cheerfully in a soddie shack.
To keep out snow, dirt, wind and rain-
They put a tar paper lean-to in back,

They fenced around the barn for cows,
Raised a flock of chickens and a dog.
Kept a gentle work horse in the big barn-
Sometimes they butchered a lean hog.

They didn't worry of fancy clothes or care
For hair pins in Grandma's white hair
Potatoes and apples filled their cellar.
Preserves in jars lined shelves in the lair.

Grandma quilted and Grandpa hunted.
They were happy on the prairie thinking,
"We are blessed with Sandhills sunshine!
And a well of pure water for drinking."

Great Grandmother Paine, Grandma Paine Nell, Elsie and Irene, my Mom probably in about 1914.

OTHER FAMILY PICTURES

Alyssa Valedictorian

Wayne, Julie, Cody and Ashley, Beth, Kristi (bride), John (groom), Kathy, Jerry, Will and Andy

Beth with some of her grandchildren

Carson with four of his great grandparents

Cowboy Caule with his daddy Cody.

Cody, Harold, Beth, Andy, Joey and Will in front

Getting ready for a family outing

Grandma and Grandpa Paine with little Webers, Jim, Lila, Ted and Beth

Grandma Beth college grad

Great grandson Treye a wrestler

Harold, Beth, Cody and Baby Ashley, May 18, 1992 (His fatal heart attack was 24 hours later!)

Jerry and Precious

Jerry shows the big tractor to Joey

Jim, Beth and Lila

Julie and Wayne on their wedding day

Kristi and Will on Prince with Andy leading

Kristi and John Snyder on their Wedding Day

Kristi and kittens

Lila and Beth volunteers at the Dawes County Museum South of Chadron.

My parents at home

Painting of Beth feeding her turkeys by Aunt Mildred

Will on Canadian Crutches

Beth's Highschool Graduation Photo

Kathy and Jerry Gibbons wedding

Airman Ashley

www.ingramcontent.com/pod-product-compliance
Lightning Source LLC
LaVergne TN
LVHW010156070526
838199LV00062B/4379